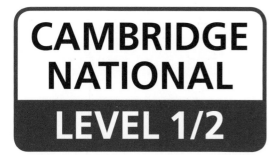

CAMBRIDGE NATIONAL
LEVEL 1/2

Enterprise and marketing

Tess Bayley
Leanna Oliver

An OCR endorsed textbook

The teaching content of this resource is endorsed by OCR for use with specification **Cambridge National Enterprise and Marketing Level 1/2 Certificate (J819)**. In order to gain OCR endorsement, this resource has been reviewed against OCR's endorsement criteria.

This resource was designed using the most up to date information from the specification. Specifications are updated over time which means there may be contradictions between the resource and the specification, therefore please use the information on the latest specification and Sample Assessment Materials at all times when ensuring students are fully prepared for their assessments.

Any references to assessment and/or assessment preparation are the publisher's interpretation of the specification requirements and are not endorsed by OCR. OCR recommends that teachers consider using a range of teaching and learning resources in preparing learners for assessment, based on their own professional judgement for their students' needs. OCR has not paid for the production of this resource, nor does OCR receive any royalties from its sale. For more information about the endorsement process, please visit the OCR website, **www.ocr.org.uk**.

Hachette UK's policy is to use papers that are natural, renewable and recyclable products and made from wood grown in well-managed forests and other controlled sources. The logging and manufacturing processes are expected to conform to the environmental regulations of the country of origin.

Orders: please contact Bookpoint Ltd, 130 Park Drive, Milton Park, Abingdon, Oxon, OX14 4SE. Telephone: +44 (0)1235 827827. Fax: +44 (0)1235 400401. Email: education@bookpoint.co.uk Lines are open from 9 a.m. to 5 p.m., Monday to Saturday, with a 24-hour message answering service. You can also order through our website: www.hoddereducation.co.uk

ISBN: 978 1 5104 5676 1

© Tess Bayley, Leanna Oliver 2019

First published in 2019 by
Hodder Education, An Hachette UK Company, Carmelite House,
50 Victoria Embankment, London EC4Y 0DZ

Impression number   10 9 8 7 6 5 4 3 2 1

Year   2023 2022 2021 2020 2019

Cover photo © peshkova – stock.adobe.com

Illustrations by Aptara Inc. and Richard Duszczak

Typeset in India by Aptara Inc.

Printed by Bell & Bain Ltd, Glasgow.

A catalogue record for this title is available from the British Library.

Contents

How to use this book

This textbook contains all three units for the Cambridge National Enterprise and Marketing Level 1/2. These are:

- Unit R064 Enterprise and marketing concepts
- Unit R065 Design a business proposal
- Unit R066 Market and pitch a business proposal

Each unit is then divided into learning outcomes. All of the teaching content for each learning outcome is covered in the book.

Key features of the book

The book is organised by the units in the qualification. Each unit is broken down into the learning outcomes from the specification. Each unit opener will help you to understand what is covered in the unit, the list of learning outcomes covered, and what you will be assessed on, fully matched to the requirements of the specification.

R064 Enterprise and marketing concepts

About this unit

This unit provides an overview and introduction to the key concepts. You will consider how a business markets its products and services to its customers, and review the internal areas that enable a business to operate successfully.

Learning outcomes

LO1 Understand how to target a market
LO2 Understand what makes a product or service financially viable
LO3 Understand product development
LO4 Understand how to attract and retain customers
LO5 Understand factors for consideration when starting up a business
LO6 Understand different functional activities needed to support a business start-up

How will I be assessed?

You will complete a 1 hour 30 minute written examination set and marked by the examination board. The examination paper will have 80 marks and will have two parts:

- Part A – 16 multiple choice questions
- Part B – short answer questions and three extended response questions.

The learning outcomes are clearly stated so you know exactly what is covered.

Assessment methods are clearly listed and fully mapped to the specification.

iv

L03 Understand product development

This learning outcome considers how businesses develop their products. Every product has a unique lifecycle and you will look at the various stages each product goes through.

Teaching content

In this learning outcome you will cover:

3.1 The product lifecycle

3.2 Extension strategies for products in the product lifecycle and the appropriateness of each

3.3 How to create product differentiation

3.4 The impact of external factors on product development

3.1 The product lifecycle

All products have a unique **product lifecycle**. However, there are five main stages that usually occur in the lifecycle of a product, as shown in Figure 1.12.

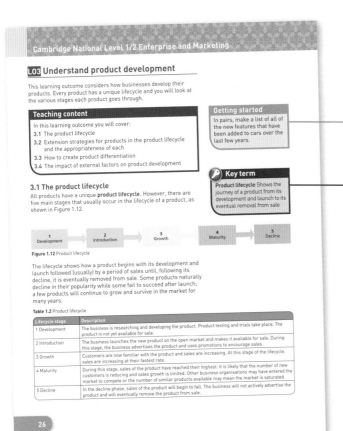

Figure 1.12 Product lifecycle

The lifecycle shows how a product begins with its development and launch followed (usually) by a period of sales until, following its decline, it is eventually removed from sale. Some products naturally decline in their popularity while some fail to succeed after launch; a few products will continue to grow and survive in the market for many years.

Table 1.2 Product lifecycle

Lifecycle stage	Description
1 Development	The business is researching and developing the product. Product testing and trials take place. The product is not yet available for sale.
2 Introduction	The business launches the new product on the open market and makes it available for sale. During this stage, the business advertises the product and uses promotions to encourage sales.
3 Growth	Customers are now familiar with the product and sales are increasing. At this stage of the lifecycle, sales are increasing at their fastest rate.
4 Maturity	During this stage, sales of the product have reached their highest. It is likely that the number of new customers is reducing and sales growth is limited. Other business organisations may have entered the market to compete or the number of similar products available may mean the market is saturated.
5 Decline	In the decline phase, sales of the product will begin to fall. The business will not actively advertise the product and will eventually remove the product from sale.

Getting started

In pairs, make a list of all of the new features that have been added to cars over the last few years.

> Short activities to introduce you to the topic.

Key term

Product lifecycle Shows the journey of a product from its development and launch to its eventual removal from sale

> Understand important terms.

26

Case study

Jamie Oliver Restaurant Group

Jamie Oliver has been in the public eye since his TV show, the *Naked Chef*, was first shown in 1999, going on to make several television series and write best-selling cookery books. His passion and enthusiasm for helping young people, through improvements to school meals, as well as setting up Fifteen, his restaurant venture to help young unemployed people back to work, has made him a popular personality.

As well as Fifteen, the Jamie Oliver Restaurant Group has a number of businesses including Jamie's Italian, Barbecoa and American diner-style restaurants.

Despite Jamie Oliver's popularity, in January 2018, Jamie's Italian closed 12 sites and asked for a cut in rent for its remaining sites. In February 2018, his Barbecoa restaurants went into administration.

So why is one of the UK's most famous and instantly recognisable chefs experiencing problems with his brand? Experts believe there are specific problems which could hinder a quick turnaround for his businesses. Questions have been asked as to whether the chef still feels the same passion for the Jamie's Italian brand, as he is now focused on his other ventures. Some believe those running the chain have tried to exploit the brand name without investing in it to keep it fresh and up-to-date, pointing out that the menu and décor of the chain have not changed since its launch.

Others believe that extremely high rents have been one of the biggest issues, pointing out that restaurants in areas such as Piccadilly and Bluewater shopping centre are among the sites that have closed. Jamie Oliver himself has blamed a 'perfect storm' of problems including high rents, increasing food costs and wages, the decline of the High Street and Brexit for the company's problems.

Questions

1 What are the main messages of this case study?

2 Research all the different products and services that are associated with Jamie Oliver. Are there any that surprise you, for example, because you did not know he was involved in that product or service?

> See how concepts can be applied to businesses and learn about real-life scenarios.

Stretch activity

1 What do you mainly associate Jamie Oliver with?

2 What advice would you give to Jamie Oliver regarding his different restaurants?

> Take your understanding and knowledge of a topic a step further with these stretch activities designed to test you, and provide you with a more in-depth understanding of the topic.

Brand identity

Figure 3.1 on page 123 shows the six main elements of brand identity, as identified by Jean-Noel Kapferer, a branding specialist.

122

v

A short task to help you understand an idea or assessment criteria. These include group and research tasks.

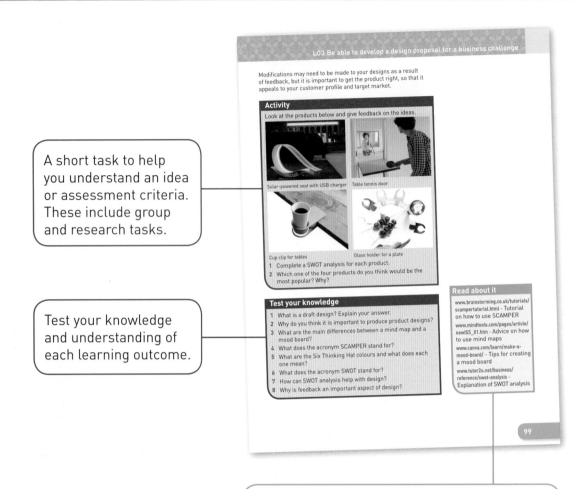

Modifications may need to be made to your designs as a result of feedback, but it is important to get the product right, so that it appeals to your customer profile and target market.

Activity

Look at the products below and give feedback on the ideas.

Solar-powered seat with USB charger

Table tennis door

Cup clip for tables

Glass holder for a plate

1 Complete a SWOT analysis for each product.
2 Which one of the four products do you think would be the most popular? Why?

Test your knowledge and understanding of each learning outcome.

Test your knowledge

1 What is a draft design? Explain your answer.
2 Why do you think it is important to produce product designs?
3 What are the main differences between a mind map and a mood board?
4 What does the acronym SCAMPER stand for?
5 What are the Six Thinking Hat colours and what does each one mean?
6 What does the acronym SWOT stand for?
7 How can SWOT analysis help with design?
8 Why is feedback an important aspect of design?

Read about it

www.brainstorming.co.uk/tutorials/scampertutorial.html – Tutorial on how to use SCAMPER

www.mindtools.com/pages/article/newISS_01.htm – Advice on how to use mind maps

www.canva.com/learn/make-a-mood-board/ – Tips for creating a mood board

www.tutor2u.net/business/reference/swot-analysis – Explanation of SWOT analysis

99

Includes references to books, websites and other sources for further reading and research.

Question practice

Part A: Multiple choice questions

1 Which of the following is an internal factor for a business?

a Customer needs

b Increased taxation rates

c New government legislation

d Staffing costs

This feature appears in Unit R064 where you will be assessed via an exam. It includes practice questions, mark schemes and example answers to help you prepare for the exam.

Acknowledgements

The Publishers would like to thank the following for permission to reproduce copyright material.

Picture credits

p. 2 © peshkova/stock.adobe.com; **p. 5** *l* © urbanbuzz/Shutterstock.com; *m* © Selwyn / Alamy Stock Photo; *r* © Chris Howes/Wild Places Photography / Alamy Stock Photo; **p. 10** © ESB Professional/Shutterstock.com; **p. 11** © georgejmclittle/stock.adobe.com; **p. 12** © Chris Brunskill/Getty Images; **p. 28** © Pamela Reynolds/Shutterstock.com; **p. 29** © Frankie Angel / Alamy Stock Photo; **p. 30** © H&M Group; **p. 40** © Innocent Drinks; **p. 41** © Art Directors & TRIP / Alamy Stock P; **p. 43** © xy/stock.adobe.com; **p. 46** © NAN/stock.adobe.com; **p. 50** © matousekfoto/stock.adobe.com; **p. 52** © Jeanette Dietl/stock.adobe.com; **p. 53** © kasto/stock.adobe. com; **p. 60** © Alterfalter/stock.adobe.com; **p. 63** © Rainer/stock.adobe.com; **p. 69** © Monkey Business/stock. adobe.com; **p. 72** © Stephen Barnes/Business / Alamy Stock Photo; **p. 73** *t* © Jeff Gilbert / Alamy Stock Photo; *b* © Halfpoint/stock.adobe.com; **p. 89** © Coca Cola; **p. 92** Science History Images / Alamy Stock Photo; **p. 93** © kyokyo/Shutterstock.com; **p. 94** © trinetuzun/stock.adobe.com; **p. 95** *t* © amenic181/stock.adobe.com; *b* © Adrian Lyon / Alamy Stock Photo; **p. 99** *tl* © Sheila Kennedy, MIT Architecture; *tr* © www.tobiasfraenzel.com; *br* © True Fabrications; *bl* © Been Kim / Drinklip / www.drinklip.com; **p. 100** © viperagp/stock.adobe.com; **p. 104** *tl* © Mark/stock.adobe.com; *tr* © Gerald Bernard/stock.adobe.com; *bl* © ronstik/stock.adobe.com; *br* © galaganov/stock.adobe.com; **p. 113** © Michael Kovac/Getty Images for The Humane Society of the United States; **p. 118** © Artur Szczybylo/Shutterstock.com; **p. 120** © Pret A Manger; **p. 121** © Mark Chivers / Alamy Stock Photo; **p. 122** © Chris Bull / Alamy Stock Photo; **p. 124** © Sk Hasan Ali/Shutterstock.com; **p. 126** © NextNewMedia/Shutterstock.com; **p. 126** *l* © Philip Hall / Alamy Stock Photo; *r* © IgorGolovniov/Shutterstock. com; **p. 128** *l* © Facebook; *m* © Shell UK Ltd; *b* © BSI group; **p. 129** *t* © Christian Vierig/Getty Images; *b* © Kirstin Sinclair/Getty Images; **p. 133** *t* © The Colin Sherborne Collection/Mary Evans Picture Library; *b* © DenisMArt/Shutterstock.com; **p. 134** *t* BedHead shampoo © razorpix / Alamy Stock Photo; *m* © Roman Tiraspolsky/123RF; *b* © Buzz Pictures / Alamy Stock Photo; **p. 135** © NikomMaelao Production/Shutterstock. com; **p. 141** © Thinglass/Shutterstock.com; **p. 142** © Sean Pavone/Shutterstock.com; **p. 143** © Ivo Antonie de Rooij/Shutterstock.com; **p. 144** © Michaelpuche/Shutterstock.com; **p. 149** © WavebreakmediaMicro/stock. adobe.com; **p. 150** © Korrawin/stock.adobe.com; **p. 156** *row 1* © Wordley Calvo Stock/stock.adobe.com; *row 2* © digitalskillet1/stock.adobe.com; *row 3* © mimagephotography/Shutterstock.com; *row 4* © olly/stock.adobe. com; *row 5* © Wayhome Studio/stock.adobe.com; **p. 157** © Djomas/Shutterstock.com; **p. 170** *l* © AlenKadr/ Shutterstock.com; *r* © DenisMArt/Shutterstock.com

Acknowledgements

p. 79: 'How M&S is getting "more bang for its buck" in marketing' – taken from article on Marketing Week website dated 24.5.17. Reprinted with permission of Centaur Media PLC.; **p. 90–91** James Dyson, inventor and designer – article from The Guardian, 24 May 2016 © Guardian News and Media. Reprinted with permission; **p. 123** JN Kapferer's identity prism from JN Kapferer, *The New Strategic Brand Management*, *5th edition* (2012), Kogan Page ed., p. 158. Reprinted with permission of JN Kapferer; **p. 139**. In Statista – The Statistics Portal. Retrieved 1 November 2018 from https://www.statista.com/statistics/629118/soft-drink-brand-ranking-in-the-united- kingdom-uk-by-convenience-sales-value/.

Every effort has been made to trace all copyright holders, but if any have been inadvertently overlooked, the Publishers will be pleased to make the necessary arrangements at the first opportunity.

Although every effort has been made to ensure that website addresses are correct at time of going to press, Hodder Education cannot be held responsible for the content of any website mentioned in this book. It is sometimes possible to find a relocated web page by typing in the address of the home page for a website in the URL window of your browser.

R064 Enterprise and marketing concepts

About this unit

This unit provides an overview and introduction to the key concepts. You will consider how a business markets its products and services to its customers, and review the internal areas that enable a business to operate successfully.

Learning outcomes

LO1 Understand how to target a market

LO2 Understand what makes a product or service financially viable

LO3 Understand product development

LO4 Understand how to attract and retain customers

LO5 Understand factors for consideration when starting up a business

LO6 Understand different functional activities needed to support a business start-up

How will I be assessed?

You will complete a 1 hour 30 minute written examination set and marked by the examination board. The examination paper will have 80 marks and will have two parts:

- Part A – 16 multiple choice questions
- Part B – short answer questions and three extended response questions.

LO1 Understand how to target a market

This learning outcome considers how a business ensures that the products and/or services it offers meet the needs and wants of its customers. You will consider how a business splits up its customers into smaller groups, often referred to as segments, and how it is able to find out what its customers want and need.

Teaching content

In this learning outcome you will cover:

1.1 The need for customer segmentation

1.2 Types of market segmentation

1.3 The benefits of market segmentation

1.4 The purpose of market research

1.5 Primary (field) market research methods (physical or digital) and their benefits

1.6 Secondary (desk) market research sources and their benefits

1.7 The types of customer feedback techniques available to business start-ups

1.1 The need for customer segmentation

Businesses sell a wide range of products and services to their customers. Together, these customers make up the **market** in which the business operates.

In order to decide which products and services to offer, a business may decide to divide the market in which it operates into groups or segments. This allows it to produce goods and services to meet the needs of each of these different segments.

In any particular market, there will be several segments. The size of these segments may be measured in terms of number of sales or the value of the sales. Not all segments are the same size: in Figure 1.1, market segment 2 is approximately twice the size of market segment 1.

Figure 1.1 Venn diagram

The particular market segment that a business plans to sell its products or services to is known as the **target market**. There are a number of reasons why businesses need to segment their markets. One key reason is that all customers are different and have their unique needs, wants and aspirations. In general, customers vary for the reasons described below.

Benefits required

Different customers require different products and services depending on their needs. For example, customers who live in warm countries such as Spain and Italy are likely to have less need for winter coats than individuals that live in colder countries, such as Norway and Iceland.

Amount of money available

Usually, depending on household income, individuals have a set amount of money they budget to spend on goods and services. For example, individuals willing to pay a large sum of money for a holiday may book an exotic cruise holiday, whereas a family with a limited budget may book a self-catering caravan holiday close to their home.

Quantity of goods required

Different customers require different quantities of goods. For instance, a family of five will need to purchase more food from the supermarket than a single person living on their own.

Quality of goods required

This often links to an individual's income. People with a high income are more likely to purchase higher quality goods than individuals on a low income. For example, a multi-millionaire may decide to purchase a new Rolls Royce car, while a family on a low income may purchase a second-hand car costing very little money.

Time and location for purchasing goods

The type of goods that a customer wishes to purchase will affect the timing and location of where the goods are purchased. For example, a person who needs a carton of milk for breakfast is likely to go early in the morning to a local store to buy the milk immediately. Individuals looking to purchase a new piece of furniture are more likely to be prepared to wait for their goods, travel further to purchase those items they really want to have in their home, and take time to consider the purchase before committing.

> **Key term**
>
> **Target market** A particular group of customers at which a good or service is aimed

1.2 Types of market segmentation

A market may be segmented by age, gender, occupation, income, geographical location and lifestyle, as outlined below.

Age

A business will offer products for sale that will appeal to individuals of particular ages. For example, a bicycle shop will sell a range of bikes of different sizes that can be used by individuals of different ages. For very young children, the shop may sell tricycles and balance bikes.

Activity

Consider how the products below are adapted to target different age groups.

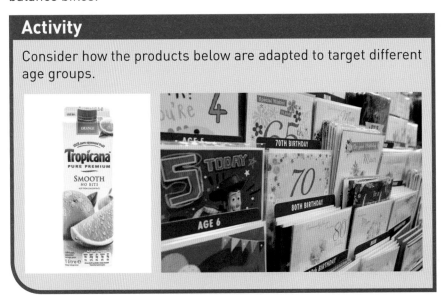

Gender

Some goods are aimed at women and others are aimed at men. Some businesses only produce products that target a particular gender, some target both genders, while others make unisex products that can be used by both men and women. These strategies help a business to increase its sales and, potentially, its profit levels.

Occupation

Businesses know that individuals from particular occupations are more likely to purchase certain goods and services. For example, teachers are known to purchase red pens for marking pupils' work; therefore, at the start of the academic year, businesses often showcase their range of 'Back to School' goods that teachers may be willing to buy.

Income

An individual's income affects their buying habits. This is often noticed when buying newspapers, holidays and cars. For example, individuals with a lower income are more likely to purchase tabloid newspapers whereas people with a higher income will purchase broadsheet newspapers.

Activity

Discuss how a shop specialising in knitwear can ensure its products appeal to both males and females.

Geographic

These markets are segmented according to where people live. Suppliers of white goods such as washing machines and tumble driers, adapt their products to meet the needs of customers based in a particular location. In Mediterranean countries, where the weather is warm, there is less demand for tumble driers and washing machines can have a slower spin speed, as clothes can be dried outside. However, in Scandinavia, higher spin speeds and tumble driers are required to ensure clothes can be dried during the long, cold winters.

Lifestyle

A person's lifestyle can be defined as their pattern of behaviour and includes their hobbies and interests. People's interests and hobbies are often based on their personal attitudes, habits and beliefs. Many businesses target individuals that have special interests, for example, an increase in the number of gyms that have opened around the country has led to a large number of sportswear and equipment shops opening.

1.3 The benefits of market segmentation

There are a number of benefits to both businesses and customers of segmenting the market.

In particular, segmentation ensures customer needs are matched and met. By focusing on one particular area, businesses are more likely to meet the needs and wants of their customers. This in turn means customers are more likely to purchase goods and therefore the business will increase sales and potentially increase its profits. If a business has segmented based on income, then it can vary the price of its goods in accordance with the target customers' income and attempt to maximise profit.

When a business focuses on its customers, it is more likely they will return to the business for their purchases. This will lead to increased **customer retention**. Businesses may encourage customers to trade up their purchases following an introductory offer, or may promote new goods to the customers when a product is coming to the end of its life.

Market (or customer) segmentation allows for targeted marketing, as a business is able to deliver its marketing and advertisements to customers who will have a key interest in the product being offered. As the business will be aware of which segment of the market to target, the right customers will be reached, and the marketing costs incurred will be less. With careful monitoring and targeting of appropriate customers, there is the potential for an increase in **market share**.

Key terms

Customer retention The ability of a business to keep customers

Market/customer segmentation The division of a market into groups or segments

Market share The section of a market controlled by a particular business

1.4 The purpose of market research

Market research is a vital part of any business success and involves finding out information about the market in which the business operates. It is vital to research the potential market when setting up a business and market research should continue to be used throughout the life of the business. Customers and the market as a whole change over time, so it is very important to undertake in-depth market research on a regular basis. This might be to assess whether new products should be introduced, existing products phased out, expansion plans should take place or, in certain circumstances, whether the business has a long-term future.

> **Key term**
>
> **Market research** The actions of a business to gather information about customers' needs and wants

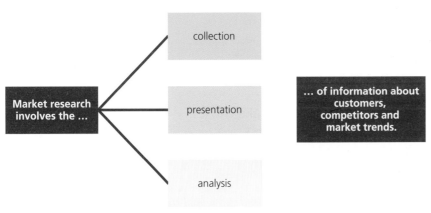

Figure 1.2 Market research

In small businesses, such as sole trader businesses, the owner often completes the market research that is required. In large companies, staff employed in marketing departments will complete market research to meet the needs of the organisation. Some businesses may also work with marketing companies or agencies who complete the market research on their behalf. Whatever their size, a business will aim to find out what existing and potential customers need and would like to buy.

Businesses complete market research for the reasons below.

Understand the market and reduce risk

Comprehensive market research will allow a business to understand the needs of the market and then provide goods and services to meet those needs. By developing a working knowledge of customer needs and wants, the business reduces the risk of making decisions about products or services that may be inaccurate and potentially costly. Although this is a major benefit of market research, many businesses opt out of the process due to the costs involved. Instead, they often try to guess what customers may want to purchase or they may just contact existing customers to try and identify changes in taste and other market trends.

To promote the organisation

By completing comprehensive market research on how a business organisation advertises and markets its products, the business organisation will be able gain vital information on what attracts customers. If the business organisation acts on the findings then they will be able to put appropriate marketing and advertising strategies in place in order to promote the business organsation's products and services.

To aid decision making

The results of detailed primary and secondary market research can be analysed at management level within a business organisation. By analysing the results in detail, a business will be able to make informed decisions based on the feedback received. This could use research on customer needs, wants and aspirations to inform decision making about the type of products or services the business organisation should provide.

Obtain customers' views

By understanding customer needs and wants, managers can make informed decisions. Market research allows customers to discuss their views, needs and wants in terms of products and services offered. Once analysed, this information provides a business with a comprehensive overview of what needs to be produced and sold in order to meet the customers' expectations. By meeting these expectations, the business is likely to maximise its sales and profits.

Inform product development and promote the business

Comprehensive and accurate market research reduces the risks involved in launching new or updated products. Whenever a business launches a new product, there is a possibility that customers will not want to buy it. Market research helps the business to reduce this risk, as it will be aware of what its customers are looking to purchase in the future. Analysed market research information will ensure that the products that are developed are up-to-date and meet the needs of customers.

A further benefit of market research is that by asking customers about their needs, the business is promoting itself to them, and this may lead to additional sales from these customers.

Introduction to types of market research

There are two main types of market research:

- **Primary research** (also known as **field research**).
- **Secondary research** (also known as **desk research**).

 Key terms

Primary (field) research Gathering data and information that has not been collected before

Secondary (desk) research Gathering data and information that has already been collected before

Table 1.1 Primary and secondary research

Type of market research and definition	Examples	Advantages	Disadvantages
Primary (field) research – gathering data and information that has not been collected before	● Interviews ● Observations ● Questionnaires ● Surveys ● Focus groups ● Consumer trials	● Relevant and up-to-date information ● The data and information are specific to the organisation completing the research ● Data and information are only available to the organisation who commissioned the research, allowing for a competitive advantage	● Costly and time consuming to complete ● A sample size that is too small may provide biased results ● Consumers are not always willing to take part in market research. They often regard telephone calls to gain information as 'nuisance calls'
Secondary (desk) research – gathering data and information that has already been collected before	● Books/trade magazines/newspapers ● Published company reports ● Internal data ● Competitors' data ● Government publications and statistics ● Purchased research material (e.g. Mintel)	● Cheaper than primary (field) research and often free, as the data and information already exists ● Information and data are frequently based on a large sample size, for example, census data ● The information and data are readily available, therefore, it is not time consuming for the business to collect it	● The information is available to all, reducing the competitive advantage to be gained ● The information and data are not specific to the business completing the analysis ● Depending on when the information was collected, it could be out of date and therefore irrelevant to the current market conditions

Factual information that is collected, for example, information about customers' ages, is known as **quantitative data**. Information about people's opinions and views is known as **qualitative data**.

> 🔑 **Key terms**
>
> **Qualitative data** Data based on the opinions of those being asked
>
> **Quantitative data** Data collected that is based on facts or numbers; it is usually easier to analyse than qualitative data

Activity

Working in pairs, categorise the following activities as either primary (field) or secondary (desk) research methods.
- Reports from the Office for National Statistics
- Internet research
- Annual financial report of a local competitor
- National newspaper article
- Focus group
- Census reports
- Observation
- Questionnaires

1.5 Primary (field) market research methods (physical or digital) and their benefits

Some of the primary market research methods outlined below may be paper based or digital/online. For example, surveys and questionnaires may involve filling in a question form, or they may be conducted online via a website, app or social media platform.

Observations

Observations involve watching and noting down what individuals do and how they behave in a particular situation. Retail stores frequently use this method, with the aim of providing the most effective and efficient store layout. However, a business must assess whether it is worth the cost outlay of completing the observation for the information that is likely to be learned.

Benefits
- If one aisle had made very few sales during the previous month, an observation may identify whether customers were avoiding the aisle entirely or just not purchasing those particular goods.

Disadvantages
- While an observation may identify what is happening, it will not provide the reasons why.
- Completing any observation is time-consuming and therefore costly.

Questionnaires

Questionnaires are a popular method of collecting primary (field) research. Questionnaires are often sent out in the post and are a set of printed or written questions usually with a choice of answers devised to collect information.

Benefits
- The information that is gained will be accurate and relevant.
- They can take place in a range of locations like personal homes, work places etc.
- Questionnaires are relatively cheap to produce.

Disadvantages:
- Many people will see the questionnaires as junk mail and place them in the bin.
- Question clarification cannot be sought as there is no one physically asking the questions.

Personal survey

A personal survey involves asking individuals questions face-to-face.

Benefits
- The information that is gained will be accurate and relevant.
- If needed, an interviewer can explain the questions to the interviewee if clarification is required.
- The survey can take place in the street, in the entrance to a store or in a pre-arranged meeting place.

Disadvantages
- Personal surveys are expensive to complete and extremely time-consuming.

Figure 1.3 Personal survey

Postal survey

In a postal survey, a large number of questionnaires are printed and distributed to individuals at their home address. Prior to distribution, the business needs to decide what sample size should be used and to whom the questionnaires should be sent. Questions must be easy to understand, well written and it must be clear what response is required. In order to achieve the best level of responses, questions tend to be short, often with multiple choices.

Benefits
● A postal survey is often cheaper than a personal survey.

Disadvantages
● It is difficult to gain any detailed answers from a postal survey.
● Many people do not respond to postal surveys as they regard them as junk mail – up to 90 per cent of these surveys will not be returned.

Telephone surveys

Many businesses now conduct telephone surveys to find out more about their customers' needs and wants. However, they must ensure they comply with the General Data Protection Regulation (GDPR) when telephoning consumers.

Benefits
● Telephone surveys allow for a wide geographical area to be covered.

Disadvantages
● Telephone surveys are relatively expensive, as they are time-consuming in terms of staff time.
● Many people fail to complete the surveys as they do not accept the telephone call or hang up when they realise what the call is about.

Internet surveys

Internet surveys are increasing popular, but the questions must be easy to read and understand, as there is no personal contact to explain their meaning. Although the internet can be used to conduct both primary and secondary research, it would not be categorised as a stand-alone research method. It is the digital tools such as websites, apps and social media that are directly used to conduct the research.

Figure 1.4 Internet survey

Benefits
● An internet survey is quick to produce and analyse.

Disadvantages
● As with telephone surveys, there is a high proportion that will be not be answered.

Focus groups

Focus groups usually provide high-quality research information. A small group of individuals are chosen, based on the needs of the business conducting the market research. These are usually

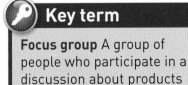

Key term

Focus group A group of people who participate in a discussion about products and services

a cross-section of the public, to ensure a wide range of views. The group then discusses key questions and themes that have been identified by the business.

Benefits
- The information gained will be accurate and relevant.
- If needed, a co-ordinator can explain the questions or direct the conversation.

Disadvantages
- Focus groups are expensive to complete and extremely time-consuming.

Consumer trials

A consumer trial is a short-term offering of a product or service that allows a limited number of consumers to examine, use or test the product before the business fully launches it. A consumer trial provides honest and reliable information and the information obtained can be used to amend the product if necessary. However, consumer trials are expensive to operate and the analysis of individuals' views and opinions is not as easy as numerical data.

Benefits
- A consumer trial provides honest and reliable information.
- The information obtained can be used to amend the product if necessary.

Disadvantages
- Consumer trials are expensive to operate.
- Analysing people's views and opinions is not as easy as analysing numerical data.

Case study

Professional football clubs are keen to provide access for all. In recent years, they have introduced focus groups to discuss with fans what their needs and wants are. As a result, the football clubs have introduced a wide range of initiatives to increase supporter enjoyment. These include fan zones that open prior to games, family areas and match day mascot opportunities.

Question

In small groups, identify a local professional sports team. Discuss potential initiatives that could be discussed during a focus group to be held with their fans.

Figure 1.5 Mascots such as Burnley Football Club's Bertie Bee are a common sight at football grounds

1.6 Secondary (desk) market research sources and their benefits

Internal data

Internal data is numerical or other data and information held by a business. When completing market research, a business must ensure it reviews all its internal information alongside any external information that is available. Businesses hold a wide range of information, for example, sales data, customer profiles and financial budgets.

Benefits
- Numerical data can be used to make predictions about the future by looking for trends over a period of time.
- Data can also be compared against local competitors or against industry benchmarks.

Disadvantages
- Internal data has a narrow scope and does not consider the wider world.

Books, newspapers and trade magazines

Books, newspapers and trade magazines may either be online or paper-based.

Benefits
- Information from these sources is relatively cheap to acquire, likely to be accurate and readily available.
- Physical books, newspapers and trade magazines can either be purchased or loaned from local libraries.

Disadvantages
- The information may be out of date, depending on publication date.
- The information collected may not be totally relevant to the business organisation.

Competitors' data

Competitors' data may be available publicly, depending on the legal structure of the business. A limited company is required by law to publish its financial data on an annual basis.

Benefits
- In the UK, this data is submitted to Companies House and is publicly available.
- By reviewing the financial records of other organisations, managers can review their own organisation's performance.

Disadvantages

- It must be remembered that for meaningful comparisons to be made data should only be compared 'like with like'. This means that a limited company should not be compared with a sole trader, for example.

Government publications and statistics

Government publications and statistics are readily available to download from the internet. Examples include the national census and publications relating to taxation such as income tax or corporation tax.

Benefits

- Government publications and statistics are generally free.
- The resources are usually readily available on the internet and comprehensive in nature.

Disadvantages

- Depending on the information required, there may be a cost.
- Although such information will be accurate and trustworthy, it may be out of date – for example, the Census is only completed every ten years.
- Any government information will be generic and not specific to the requirements and situation of the business downloading the information.

Purchased research material

Market research companies such as Mintel sell research material to businesses. Examples include Mintel's reports on cause marketing, marketing to sports fans and sports and enrgy drinks. Before purchasing such information, a business should consider the likely usefulness of the material, by considering the following:

- What will this purchased report tell us?
- Can we purchase only the part of the report that is relevant to us?
- Who is the author?
- When was the report written?
- Which report is best for the business?

Benefits

- This research material is readily available on the internet and comprehensive in nature.

Disadvantages

- Depending on the information required, there may be a cost.
- As with other secondary (desk) research, it must be remembered that the information could be out of date and not totally relevant to the particular circumstances being considered.

Activity

A new fast food restaurant is opening in Northern Town. Copy and complete the tables to advise the owners of the most appropriate primary (field) and secondary (desk) research methods to gain market information.

Primary (field) research methods that could be used by the new fast food restaurant	Description of primary (field) research method	Advantages of primary (field) research method	Disadvantages of primary (field) research method

Secondary (desk) research methods that could be used by the new fast food restaurant	Description of secondary (desk) research method	Advantages of secondary (desk) research method	Disadvantages of secondary (desk) research method

1.7 The types of customer feedback techniques available to business start-ups

When completing market research, a business organisation needs to consider how it will receive feedback from its customers. In recent years, many businesses are keen to send online surveys to their customers to review their experience. Hotels are keen to do this and often send guests forms to review their stay after leaving. Motor garages frequently telephone their customers to review the services offered during a visit to the dealership. Smaller business organisations often have comment cards where customers can leave opinions and views about customer service.

By making customer service measurements, a business organisation will be able to:

1 Make informed decisions about its future product developments. By having detailed information about what customers need and want, business organisations can develop products to meet these needs.

2 Retain customers. Business organisations that meet and respond to their customers' needs will ensure that customers will return to their business and purchase goods from them in the future.

3 Remain competitive. By meeting customers' needs and listening to what customers think of their products and services, a business organisation is able to continue to make sales and therefore remain competitive in the market.

4 Identify areas of strengths and weaknesses. By asking customers for their opinions both positive and negative, a business organisation is able to identify its key strengths and weaknesses.

Business organisations have to make a decision about how to receive feedback from their customers. The following are the main techniques used by business organisations:

● **Repeat business data** – the number of customers that return to the business to purchase their goods and services.

● The number of **complaints/compliments** gathered over a period of time.

● **Mystery shoppers** – individuals who enter a business organisation to make a purchase and then review the performance of the business organisation on how they were treated and served.

● **Social media/online communities** with reviews and comments – social media platforms such as Facebook and Twitter allow customers to comment and review their experiences of different business organisations.

● **Online surveys** – online surveys are increasingly popular and are sent to customers to review a business organisation's performance. When preparing any internet survey, the questions must be easy to read and understand, as there is no personal contact to explain meanings.

● **Customer comment cards** – these are cards/pieces of paper that are left in business organisations on which customers can make comments and return to a member of staff or sealed box and can be reviewed by management at a later time.

● **Comments made to staff members** – customers may make comments to staff members about a business organisation's performance. These comments are then passed to management to make informed decisions.

● **Telephone/email surveys** – many business organisations in recent years have started to use telephone and email surveys to gather information. It is important to remember that business organisations must comply with data protection legislation when telephoning customers.

● **Email contact forms** – contact forms are used by business organisations to gather information and collect customer data. Once the information has been collected, business organisations can send marketing and product information to their customers.

Customer feedback is very important to new business organisations. Without having a clear understanding of what customers need and want, a new business organisation is unlikely to succeed. For example, an entrepreneur considering opening a new indoor children's play area would be likely to conduct primary and secondary research. They could:

- ask parents of young children to complete questionnaires
- conduct focus groups in local primary schools
- use the internet to review the number of other play areas in the local area
- research national statistics to find out the number of children in the target area
- visit competitor play areas, to ascertain what activities and facilities are currently being offered.

Read about it

www.businesslink.co.uk – provides practical examples on how to be a successful business person.

www.socialenterprise.org.uk – a national body for social enterprise which provides excellent practical examples

Test your knowledge

1 Define the term market research.
2 Identify five sources of primary (field) research.
3 Identify five types of market segmentation.
4 Explain the advantages of a business organisation segmenting its customers.
5 Assess the benefits of an existing business conducting primary (field) and secondary (desk) research.

Activity

In small groups, discuss how a hotel may receive feedback from its guests about the services offered.

Stretch activity

Analyse why it is important for a new business organisation to identify and research its target market.

L02 Understand what makes a product or service financially viable

This learning outcome will enable you to understand the different types of costs that are incurred when producing a product or service. You will be able to practise numerical questions to gain an appreciation of how data is used by business organisations to make informed decisions.

Teaching content

In this learning outcome you will cover:

2.1 Cost of producing the product or service

2.2 Revenue generated by sales of the product or service

2.3 Use of break-even as an aid to decision making

2.4 Profit level

Getting started

Working in small groups, consider a local bakery. Make a list of all of the costs the bakery will need to pay when producing and selling its bread, cakes and pastries.

2.1 Cost of producing the product or service

Costs are expenses that businesses incur when producing and selling their different products and services. There are a number of ways of categorising these costs.

Fixed costs

Fixed costs are costs that remain unchanged when the output of a business organisation changes. For example, the rental costs of a clothing factory will not change regardless of whether the factory makes 10 items of clothing or 100 items of clothing. Even when the factory is closed, the rental costs remain unchanged.

Examples of fixed costs include:

- rent of business premises
- loan repayments made to financial institutions
- advertising of products and services
- insurance, e.g. of the buildings and the building contents
- salaries and wages paid to employees
- utilities such as electricity and water.

A graph of fixed costs will show a straight line (see Figure 1.6).

Although fixed costs do not vary with output, they will not always remain constant. For example, employees' salaries and electricity costs may go up, but the costs will be fixed with respect to the level of output.

Fixed costs will usually increase when a business organisation is working at full capacity. For example, if a clothes manufacturer requires extra factory space to produce its goods, its rental costs

Key terms

Fixed costs Costs that remain unchanged when the output of a business changes

Variable costs Costs that vary directly with (and are dependent on) the level of output

Figure 1.6 Fixed costs

will suddenly increase. These increases are known as stepped costs and can be seen on a graph of fixed costs (see Figure 1.7).

Variable costs

Variable costs vary directly with the level of output. This means that the costs are totally dependent on the level of output.

Examples of variable costs include:

- stock – also known as inventory, this is the goods or items that a business organisation keeps in its shop or warehouse for sale. For example, a sandwich shop may have bags of crisps and bottles of drink available to sell to its customers.
- raw materials – these are the basic resources that a product is made from. For example, a sandwich shop would have bread, butter, meat and salad as its raw materials.
- components – these are parts that make up a whole item. For example, in making a bread roll, flour would be a component.
- packaging costs – these are the costs in packaging the finished products. For example, the costs of putting the finished sandwiches into boxes for sale.

Consider the example of the clothes factory again: if production of clothing doubles, then the variable costs double; if production of clothing halves, the variable costs halve; if output is zero, then no variable costs are incurred. The formula for working out variable costs is shown below.

Total variable costs = Variable cost per unit × Output level

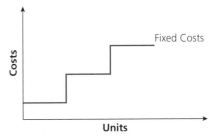

Figure 1.7 Stepped costs

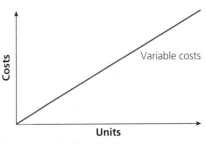

Figure 1.8 Variable costs

Activity

Consider your local supermarket.
1 Make a list of the costs the supermarket will incur during one year.
2 Categorise these costs as either fixed or variable costs.

Note: Some costs, such as salaries and utilities, can be classified as either fixed costs or variable costs. However, for the Cambridge National in Enterprise and Marketing qualification, both of these are counted as fixed costs, while wages are classified as a variable cost.

Total costs

Total costs are calculated by adding together all of the business's costs for a particular level of output.

For example, when the clothing factory produces 100 items of clothing, the total cost would be the factory's fixed costs plus its variable costs for these 100 items of clothing. If no items of clothing are sold, then the total costs would just consist of fixed costs.

Key term

Total costs Calculated by adding together all the business's costs for a particular level of output

The formula for working out total costs is:

Total costs = Fixed costs + Variable costs

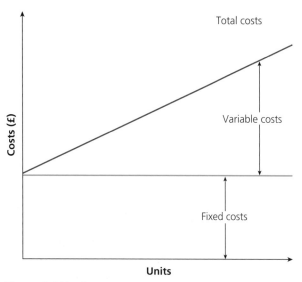

Figure 1.9 Total costs

Activity

Sunny Beach Supplies sells bucket and spades to holiday makers in Scarborough. The owner, Jim, has provided the following information:

For an output level of 100 buckets and spades, the fixed costs are £3 000 and the variable costs are £500.

1   Calculate total costs for an output of 100 buckets and spades.
2   Calculate the variable cost for one bucket and spade.
3   Calculate total costs if output increased to 150 buckets and spades.

2.2 Revenue generated by sales of the product or service

How to calculate total revenue

Revenue is defined as the money that a business earns from selling goods or providing services.

The **total revenue** a business earns is found by multiplying the selling price of the goods by the number of good sold:

Total revenue = Selling price per unit x Number of sales

For example, if the clothing manufacturer sells 100 jumpers at £10.00 each, the total revenue will be 100 × £10 = £1,000.

 Key terms

Revenue The money a business earns from selling goods or providing services

Total revenue The total amount of money earned at a particular output level. It is calculated as selling price per unit × output level (number of sales)

Activity

Copy the table and fill in the gaps to complete the sales and revenue data for an office retailer.

Product	Selling price per unit (£)	Number of sales	Total revenue (£)
Table	150.00	1 000	?
Chair	75.00	5 000	?
Filing cabinet	250.00	200	?
Bookshelf	?	300	3 000
Storage unit	500.00	?	5 000
Laptop	550.00	350	?
Stationery set	5.00	3 500	?

2.3 Use of break-even as an aid to decision making

Many business organisations want to maximise the **profits** they make. There are a few exceptions where this does not apply, for example a local sports club may be non-profit-making and only exists to provide services to its members.

A profit is a financial gain. It is calculated as the difference between the total revenue and total costs.

Owners need to remember that there is always the possibility their business will not make a profit. For example, new businesses, small businesses and those struggling in a difficult economic environment may find it hard to generate any profits at all. In these cases, a business organisation may simply aim to **break-even**.

Definition of break-even

Break-even is the level of output at which total costs equal total revenue. At this point a business makes no profit and no loss.

A business is able to calculate the number of sales it needs to make in order to break-even each year. Whenever a business calculates its break-even point, there are a number of assumptions that have to be made:

- all output that has been made is sold
- there is no inventory (stock) left unsold
- only one type of product is made by the business organisation
- all costs are categorised as either fixed costs or variable costs.

There are two possible ways of calculating the break-even point:

- break-even formula
- break-even graph.

Key terms

Profit A financial gain. Profit is calculated as the difference between total revenue and total costs

Break-even The point at which a business makes no profit and no loss. It is the point at which total costs equal total revenue

Stretch activity

1. Use the internet to research a business that has appeared in the news because it has failed to make any profit.

2. Working in small groups, discuss the business's strategies for increasing its profit.

Break-even formula

The formula for break-even is:

$$\text{Break-even point (in units)} = \frac{\text{Fixed costs}}{\text{Selling price per unit} - \text{Variable cost per unit}}$$

Contribution is the amount left over after variable costs have been subtracted from sales revenue. Contribution per unit is calculated as selling price per unit minus variable cost per unit. This means that the break-even formula can also be written as:

$$\text{Break-even point (in units)} = \frac{\text{Fixed costs}}{\text{Contribution per unit}}$$

Contribution is different to profit, as fixed costs are not subtracted from the selling price.

 Key term

Contribution The amount left over after variable costs have been subtracted from sales revenue. Contribution per unit is calculated as selling price per unit minus variable cost per unit

Activity

Complete the table to calculate contribution per unit and break-even point in units.

The first row has been completed as an example.

	Total fixed costs	Selling price per unit	Variable costs per unit	Contribution per unit	Break-even point in units
	£	£	£	£	Units
1	60 000	20	10	20 – 10 = 10	60 000 ÷ 10 = 6 000 units
2	240 000	100	60		
3	600 000	25	15		
4	500 000	36	11		
5	3 000 000	250	150		
6	500 000	500	300		
7	500 000	300	200		
8	300 000	250	150		
9	300 000	150	50		
10	900 000	450	200		

Break-even graphs

It is also possible to calculate the break-even point and present it in a graph (see Figure 1.10).

When drawing a break-even graph, three lines need to plotted and drawn:

- Fixed costs
- Total costs
- Total revenue

The break-even point is the point at which the total revenue and total costs lines cross.

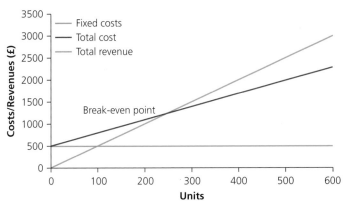

Figure 1.10 Break-even point

The fixed cost line on the graph above is a straight horizontal line because costs remain unchanged as the output level of a firm changes. It does not matter what level of output the firm produces (even zero output makes no difference); any cost which is a fixed cost will remain the same.

Total costs are calculated by adding fixed costs to variable costs. Therefore, the total cost line will start at the same point as the fixed cost line. It will then follow the same shape as a variable cost line.

Varying directly, in the case of variable costs, means that the total variable cost will be totally dependent on the level of output. If output doubles, then the variable cost would double. If halved, the variable costs would halve. If output was zero, then no variable costs would be incurred. An example can be seen in the diagram below:

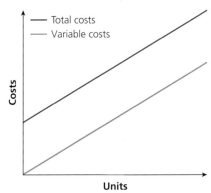

Figure 1.11 Impact of variable costs on total costs

The total revenue line represents the revenue earned from selling output. It is based on both the level of output and the selling price of this output.

The break-even number of sales that a business organisation needs to gain is found by looking at the point at which the total revenue line crosses the total cost line.

Case study

Snuffie Dog Apparel sells luxury dog collars and leads. The owner, Phil, has prepared the following table of costs based on varying levels of output.

You are required to help Phil work out the missing figures. The first line has been completed as an example.

Output of collars and leads	Variable cost per collar and lead	Total variable costs	Total fixed costs	Total costs
Units	£	£	£	£
20 000	5	100 000 (20 000 x 5)	250 000	350 000 (100 000 + 250 000)
30 000	5		250 000	
50 000	5		250 000	
75 000	3		250 000	
90 000		270 000	250 000	
100 000	2.50			
150 000			250 000	

How break-even information is used

Break-even information is used by a business to determine how many units it needs to sell in order to cover its costs and not make a loss.

Accountants may use break-even information to see how different sales levels will affect an organisation's profits. By determining how much should be sold, targets can be set for the sales team.

When launching a new business or trying to secure finance, a business owner may calculate break-even information in order to persuade a bank to lend money. Break-even information can form part of a business plan.

Stretch activity

Wooden Toys Ltd produces high-quality rocking horses to sell in the UK. Each rocking horse sells for £250.00 and the company plans to produce and sell 2 000 rocking horses each year.

Using the data in the table, prepare a break-even graph to calculate the number of rocking horses Wooden Toys Ltd need to sell in order to break-even.

Cost per rocking horse	£
Raw materials	90.00
Components	10.00
Direct labour	60.00
Fixed costs	30.00

2.4 Profit level

Most businesses exist to make a profit. Profit is the business owners' reward for investing in the business organisation.

Calculating profit per unit

Businesses often want to know how much profit a particular product or service is making. The calculation for this is:

Selling price (revenue) per unit – Total cost per unit = Profit or loss per unit

(Remember: Total costs per unit = Fixed costs per unit + Variable costs per unit.)

Calculating profit for a given level of output

The calculation to find out profit for a given level of output is:

Sales revenue – Total costs = Profit or loss

Cash flow

Cash flow is the movement of money in and out of a business. Cash comes into a business organisation in the form of receipts, known as cash inflows. These receipts could be from taking out a loan or mortgage or from selling goods to customers.

Cash goes out of a business in the form of payments, known as cash outflows. These payments could include wages, salaries, utilities and raw materials.

Net cash flow is calculated as cash inflow minus cash outflow:

Net cash flow = Cash inflow – Cash outflow

Cash flow is different to profit as cash flow only relates to money coming in and out of a business organisation, whereas the calculation of total profit includes other items.

Key term

Cash flow The movement of money in and out of a business

Read about it

www.peterjones.com – provides information about Peter Jones as an entrepreneur and includes short video clips.

www.bbc.co.uk/news/business – up to date news articles relating to business and the current economic climate.

www.gov.uk/browse/tax – information from the UK Government, including key taxation details.

http://europa.eu – up to date information about the European Union.

Test your knowledge

1 Explain the difference between fixed and variable costs.
2 Identify three fixed and three variable costs.
3 Define the term 'break-even point'.
4 Explain the difference between contribution and profit.
5 Discuss why a business may produce a break-even graph.
6 Calculate the total costs if sales revenue is £300 000 and profit is £50 000.

L03 Understand product development

This learning outcome considers how businesses develop their products. Every product has a unique lifecycle and you will look at the various stages each product goes through.

Teaching content

In this learning outcome you will cover:

3.1 The product lifecycle

3.2 Extension strategies for products in the product lifecycle and the appropriateness of each

3.3 How to create product differentiation

3.4 The impact of external factors on product development

Getting started

In pairs, make a list of all of the new features that have been added to cars over the last few years.

🔑 Key term

Product lifecycle Shows the journey of a product from its development and launch to its eventual removal from sale

3.1 The product lifecycle

All products have a unique **product lifecycle**. However, there are five main stages that usually occur in the lifecycle of a product, as shown in Figure 1.12.

| 1 Development | 2 Introduction | 3 Growth | 4 Maturity | 5 Decline |

Figure 1.12 Product lifecycle

The lifecycle shows how a product begins with its development and launch followed (usually) by a period of sales until, following its decline, it is eventually removed from sale. Some products naturally decline in their popularity while some fail to succeed after launch; a few products will continue to grow and survive in the market for many years.

Table 1.2 Product lifecycle

Lifecycle stage	Description
1 Development	The business is researching and developing the product. Product testing and trials take place. The product is not yet available for sale.
2 Introduction	The business launches the new product on the open market and makes it available for sale. During this stage, the business advertises the product and uses promotions to encourage sales.
3 Growth	Customers are now familiar with the product and sales are increasing. At this stage of the lifecycle, sales are increasing at their fastest rate.
4 Maturity	During this stage, sales of the product have reached their highest. It is likely that the number of new customers is reducing and sales growth is limited. Other business organisations may have entered the market to compete or the number of similar products available may mean the market is saturated.
5 Decline	In the decline phase, sales of the product will begin to fall. The business will not actively advertise the product and will eventually remove the product from sale.

A product lifecycle is usually represented on a graph like the one in Figure 1.13.

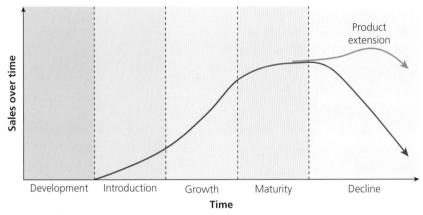
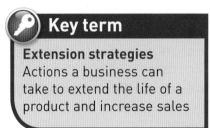

Figure 1.13 Product lifecycle graph

Extension strategies

As a product reaches the end of the maturity stage of the product lifecycle, a business may try to extend its life by incorporating new **extension strategies**, for example, designing a new model, offering new flavours/colours or changing the packaging. This may encourage new customers to purchase the product and existing customers to continue to purchase. You will look at different types of extension strategy in the next section.

Key term

Extension strategies
Actions a business can take to extend the life of a product and increase sales

Activity

Copy out the product lifestyle diagram below and fill in the labels

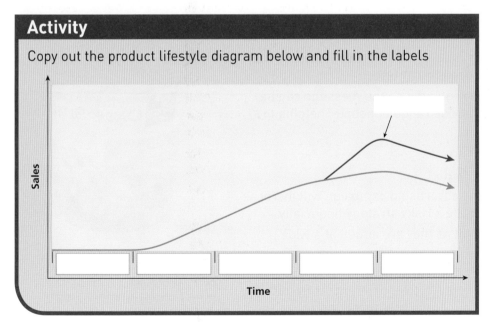

Stretch activity

1 Identify the stages of a product lifecycle for a mobile phone.
2 In pairs, discuss how long each of the different stages may be and when the manufacturer is likely to introduce a new model.

3.2 Extension strategies for products in the product lifecycle and the appropriateness of each

It is often cheaper for a business to make changes to an existing product than to develop a brand-new product for sale. With this in mind, businesses do all they can to extend the growth and maturity phases of successful products.

There are a number of different strategies that can be used to extend the life of a product.

Advertising

A business may undertake a new advertising campaign for its product.

Benefits

- A successful advertising campaign can be an effective way of attracting new customers, as well as reminding existing customers of how good the product is.
- Advertising can be used to draw attention to new 'added value' features for an existing product. For example, porridge is popular but is viewed as time-consuming to make. This has led to the introduction of microwaveable porridge pots that consumers can prepare quickly at home or at work as the pot has a pre-measured amount and only needs boiling water.
- Effective advertising has a wide coverage meaning that a lot of different people will see the advertisements.
- The business will have full control of the advertisements, so they can ensure the correct message is portrayed.
- Advertisements are repeated regularly, so the message can be effectively communicated to a wide range of people, helping to build brand loyalty.

Disadvantages

- Advertising costs can be very high.
- There is no guarantee that the advertising campaign will increase sales of the product, so it may be a risky strategy financially.
- Advertisements are impersonal as they are aimed at a wide range of people.
- Advertisements are a one-way form of communication and lack flexibility. They cannot be adjusted to take different views into account and do not allow customers to ask questions.

Figure 1.14 Quaker Oat So Simple porridge pots are advertised as a quick and easy version of traditional porridge

Price changes

A business organisation may decide to increase or reduce the price of its product.

Benefits

- Raising the price of a product will increase revenue and therefore make more profit for a business organisation.
- Increasing the price alongside a re-branding of the product may allow a business to enter the luxury market, where people are prepared to pay more for products. This means the business will increase its profits when selling the same number of goods.
- Reducing the price of a product will often make it more attractive to both new and existing customers.

Disadvantages

- An increase in product price may mean that customers will buy their products from another retailer, if they feel that the increased price is not in line with that charged by competitors.
- An increase in product price is likely to mean that customers will expect a better quality product. If this is not the case, a business may see a reduction in sales.
- Reducing the price of a product too much can devalue a product and make it seem worthless. This would mean customers would be unwilling to purchase the product.
- A cut in the price of an existing product will reduce the amount of profit the business makes per unit. It would therefore need to sell extra products in order to cover the loss in revenue.

Adding value

This is a popular strategy which involves the business adding new features to an existing product; for example, adding extra memory to a mobile phone or creating a cordless version of a vacuum cleaner.

Benefits

- This strategy works well for brands that are well known and have been popular for many years.
- By adding value, a business can charge customers more for their products. This leads to increased revenue and therefore profitability.
- A business can add value by making premium products to differentiate itself from its competitors. This may help it attract new and additional customers.

Disadvantages

- Re-launching an existing product can be costly, requiring considerable financial investment in terms of research, piloting, trialling and then marketing the updated product.
- Adding value will not be successful if there is no demand for the original product. Before deciding to add value to an existing product, a business will often carry out research to check there is likely to still be demand for the product in the future.

Figure 1.15 New cordless models of Dyson vacuum cleaners are an example of existing products with added value

Exploration of new markets

If a business is selling a product that has universal appeal but has yet to target a full range of customers, it could decide to sell its product in new markets. For example, a business that currently only sells its products in a particular region may decide to sell products throughout the country; a business that produces adult clothing may decide to introduce a children's range.

Benefits

- If a business can successfully tap into a new market, it may see its sales – and therefore profits – increase considerably.
- There is the possibility that by exploring new markets, the benefits gained will balance out the risks of current investment.
- By exploring new markets, an alternative is available when an existing market starts to decline.

Disadvantages

- This strategy may not be suitable for every product. Certain products may only be popular in certain geographic locations, for example, kilts may be popular in Scotland but will have a limited market in Wales.
- Exploration into new markets may need staff to have new skills – this could be expensive and increase costs.

Figure 1.16 H&M have extended their brand by moving into homewares

New packaging

This can be a relatively cheap method of updating a product. A business will refresh a products current packaging by changing the colours or logos, etc., in order to encourage customers to continue to purchase the product. Many companies change the packaging of their products by offering versions to tie in with particular themes, such as Christmas, Halloween or Easter, or by offering versions that tie-in with newly-released films.

Benefits

- If a business provides improved packaging, customers may perceive an increase in quality and therefore be prepared to pay a higher price.
- Newly-designed packaging may attract new customers and increase the number of sales.

Disadvantages

- Packaging design can be expensive and, depending on the type of product or service, may have a short life. For example, packaging introduced to coincide with a new film launch can only be used for a relatively short period of time.

Activity

The technology industry is known for the fast pace at which new and improved product versions are introduced.

Choose one type of product, such as a games console, computer or mobile phone, etc. Working in small groups, discuss the different extension strategies that have been used to extend the life of your chosen product.

Case study

Ryder Golf and Sports Equipment has developed a fitness band called 'Golf IT' that is worn by golfers to record how far they have walked around the golf course. In the last two years, the business has had very little sales growth and in the last six months, sales have started to decline.

Questions

1 Consider what extension strategies Ryder Golf and Sports Equipment could use to extend the life of the Golf IT.

2 Review the advantages and disadvantages of each of the strategies suggested.

3.3 How to create product differentiation

In order for a business to be successful, it must ensure that it differentiates its products or services by making sure they stand out from those of its rivals.

Establishing a strong brand image

One way of creating product differentiation is to establish a strong brand image. Business organisations create strong brand images in a number of ways. These will vary depending on the type of business, but may include sustained advertising campaigns, sponsorship of sports/music events and the importance of ensuring the availability of the product in many markets.

Many businesses, for example, McDonalds, have a very strong brand image – one that is instantly recognisable around the world. Customers know exactly what is sold by McDonalds and the company takes care to ensure its products remain the same no matter where in the world they are purchased.

Benefits

● The business name is enough to sell its goods or services without it needing to do anything else to make its product different from those of rivals.

Disadvantages

● The cost of developing a strong brand image can be extremely high. This may reduce profits if the strategy is unsuccessful.

● Developing a strong brand image takes a very long time. This is not a short-term strategy for a business.

Identifying a clear unique selling point (USP)

Many businesses develop a **unique selling point (USP)**. This is a product feature that separates the product from its competitors. There are a number of examples of products with identifiable USPs in the market today, for example:

- car performance – Audi (the slogan 'Innovation through technology')
- sports branding – Nike (the 'swoosh' and the slogan 'Just do it')
- design – Apple iPhone and iPod.

Advantages
- The name of the business sells the goods or services without it needing to make its products different from those of rivals.
- As with developing a strong brand image, identifying a clear USP takes a very long time. This is not a short-term strategy for a business.

Disadvantages
- The costs of developing a clear USP can be extremely high. However, once established, the USP should repay the costs that were initially incurred.

Improved offering

Sometimes a business decides it needs to differentiate itself further and will decide to make improvements to its current product offering. This might involve changing a products:

- location – this could be the location of a product in a particular store or the geographical location of where products are sold. For example, a supermarket may place a product at the end of an aisle facing customers as they enter the store, in order to attract their attention
- features and **functions** – adding extra features and functions to products and locations. For example, a number of fast food restaurants now offer drive-through facilities, table service or the option to order from an onscreen menu
- design and appearance – many stores have 'face lifts' to increase their appeal
- offer – a supermarket may add a café or pharmacy
- current selling price – to try to give an increased sense of perceived value, a business may reduce the selling price of its products and services.

Advantages
- It can be relatively easy and cheap to make small changes to the design and appearance of a product.

Key term

Unique selling point (USP) The key features that make a product or service different to others in the market

Key term

Function The job which a product or service is designed to do

- Increasing the selling price can increase revenue and profitability, while reducing the price may lead to an increased sense of value for money and therefore, higher sales.
- Improving the offer of a business usually increases brand image and loyalty.

Disadvantages

- Changes to a product's location, features or functions may be expensive to implement.
- Market research would need to be undertaken before deciding to make changes, as the costs involved could reduce profits.

Design mix model

A number of businesses use a design mix model – this is a way of considering the variables that contribute to successful product design. These variables are:

- function – a product must be able to do the job for which it is designed
- cost – a product must be financially viable and cost effective to produce. This means using materials that are most appropriate to the product in terms of what it is required to do and ensuring appropriate manufacturing costs (known as **economic manufacture**)
- appearance – how a product looks and feels may be very important and is referred to as its **aesthetics**.

Figure 1.17 shows a traditional product design mix.

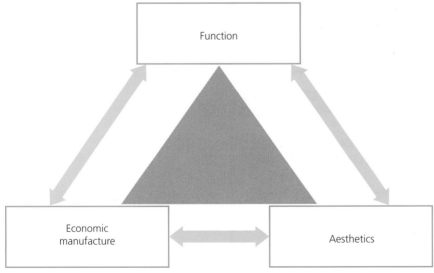

Figure 1.17 The design mix model

 Key terms

Economic manufacture Making sure the costs involved in producing a product are appropriate to that product and no money is wasted during the manufacturing process

Aesthetics How a product looks or feels

Different businesses will prioritise different areas of the design mix for a product, depending on the type of product they are producing and type of customer they are aiming at.

For example, Figure 1.18 shows how a washing machine manufacturer would focus on the function element of the design mix model (1 in the diagram), whereas a luxury handbag design company would focus on the aesthetics of the bags it designs (2 in the diagram).

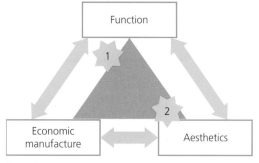

Figure 1.18 Placing products in the design mix

Activity

Copy the design mix model above. Place the following products where you think they belong in the design mix. Compare your decisions with another class member.

1 Rolls Royce car
2 McDonalds Happy Meal
3 Apple iPod
4 Computer desk
5 Gold watch
6 Supermarket value chicken
7 Underground train

Activity

The airline industry has changed rapidly in recent years, with varying levels of service and price being introduced to meet the needs of different customers. Low cost and budget airlines have had a big impact on the market, which was once dominated by large airlines such as British Airways, Virgin and United Airlines.

1 Discuss in small groups how different airlines differentiate themselves against their competitors. In your discussion consider brand image, USP, improving the offering and the design mix model.

2 Consider the advantages and disadvantages of each of the different ways used to differentiate an airline.

Each member of the group needs to think about how a chosen airline would meet their own particular needs.

3.4 The impact of external factors on product development

When developing any product, a business must consider those issues that will be outside of its control. These fall into three main categories – technological, economic and legal – as outlined below.

Technological developments

Technological developments occur all the time, so a new product that contains electronic components must be able to deal with advances in technology if it is to remain relevant. For example, many televisions are now advertised as being '4K ready' so that when this new technology becomes more widespread the televisions will still be relevant.

It is important to remember that technological issues may relate to either the business's products or to prospective consumers. For example, consumers often want to purchase the most up-to-date versions of a product. This is especially true where mobile phones or computer tablets are concerned as there is then very little demand for the previous models.

Businesses need to ensure their products incorporate all the latest features expected by the customer – carrying out customer research and then developing new features to meet these needs is likely to be costly. A business may need to invest in new machinery or factories to produce the new models as well as invest in training staff to manufacture and sell the new models. They may also need to sell off older stock at a much-reduced price that is now out of date and less appealing to customers.

Economic issues

No organisation exists in isolation – a business must take account of the current economic climate and adapt accordingly. The economic cycle in most developed countries is one of recession followed by growth, followed by boom followed by downturn followed by growth, and so on. Figure 1.19 provides an illustration of this economic cycle, which is referred to as the business cycle.

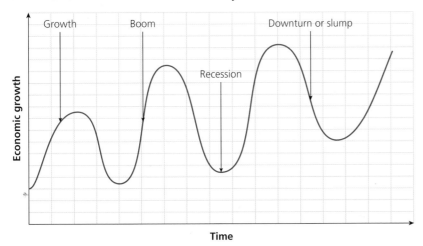

Figure 1.19 The business cycle

- During a downturn, businesses suffer from a decrease in sales and there is little or no demand for new products or services. A business is unlikely to develop new products during this time.
- During period of economic growth, customers have more money to spend and are likely to want to purchase new goods or services. Businesses will therefore develop and sell new products.
- During the boom period, customer spending is at its highest and businesses are likely to introduce and sell a wide range of new products.
- During a recession, customers have very little money to spend on luxury goods, so businesses will consider developing cheaper products or reducing the range of products they produce.

Legal issues

When developing any product, a business must comply with all current legislation, especially in relation to safety standards. Legislation is created by UK government or the European Union. A business is likely to be affected by product safety standards.

Product Safety Standards

These are the technical and legal requirements that are in place to ensure that products that are produced are safe for use and fit for purpose. The government produces guidance and legislation on the safety, design, packaging and insurance of products. For example, there are strict guidelines on the safe production and sale of fireworks.

Copyright and patents

Business organisations must ensure that they comply with laws relating to **copyright** and **patents**. Copyright protects ownership of original pieces of creative and intellectual work, such as music and books, whereas a patent protects new inventions from being used or produced by others. When developing a new product, a business could apply for a patent or copyright to ensure that its idea is not copied. However, the business must also ensure that it does not reproduce ideas belonging to others.

 Key terms

Copyright Provides legal ownership to original pieces of creative work

Patent Provides legal ownership of new inventions and prevents these being used or produced by others

Test your knowledge

1. Identify and describe the main stages of the product lifecycle.
2. Explain two extension strategies that could be used to extend the life of a product.
3. Define the term 'unique selling point'. Provide an example to illustrate your answer.
4. Explain how a business may use the design mix model.
5. Describe how each of the stages of the business cycle (recession, growth, boom and decline) may affect the success of a new product launch.

Activity

Choose a business with which you are familiar. How has your chosen business changed over the last few years to adapt to changes in the economic environment?

LO4 Understand how to attract and retain customers

This learning outcome considers how businesses attract and retain their customers. It will look at both financial and non-financial methods of gaining new customers and also retaining existing customers.

Teaching content

In this learning outcome you will cover:

4.1 Factors to consider when pricing a product to attract and retain customers

4.2 Types of pricing strategies and the appropriateness of each

4.3 Types of advertising methods used to attract and retain customers and the appropriateness of each

4.4 Sales promotion techniques used to attract and retain customers and the appropriateness of each

4.5 How customer service is used to attract and retain customers

Getting started

Think about the shop windows and advertisements that you have seen in local stores.

List all of the different pricing strategies used to encourage you to buy different products, which you have seen.

4.1 Factors to consider when pricing a product to attract and retain customers

When pricing a product, a business will make an informed decision based on its market research and the factors explained below.

Cost of production

In general terms, a business will price its product by working out what it costs to buy or make the product and then adding the amount of profit it would like to make (Figure 1.20). There is little point selling a product for a lower price that it has cost to produce as the business would make a loss.

Product costs + Profit = Selling price

Figure 1.20 Working out a selling price

Income levels of target customers

When deciding on price, a business will also need to understand the income level of its target customers. For example, luxury car makers can charge high prices as their potential customers will earn a high salary. Budget supermarkets will charge low prices as many of their customers will have a low income.

Price of competitor products

If a competitor is already selling a similar product, it will be difficult to sell another product for a price that is higher than that of the competitor because customers tend to chooser the cheaper option. If a business needs to lower the price of its products in order to compete, this will have a significant impact on its profits.

Larger businesses often have more bargaining power and can usually achieve lower production costs – these advantages are referred to as economies of scale. This means that larger businesses are able to sell at a more competitive (lower) price than smaller businesses.

It is important to remember that when lowering the cost of any product, careful consideration must be given to the effect on both production costs and overall profits.

4.2 Types of pricing strategies and the appropriateness of each

There are a number of pricing strategies a business organisation can adopt when selling to customers, as shown in Table 1.3.

Key terms

Competitive pricing Setting a price that is similar to that of a local competitor

Price skimming Introducing a product at a high price then gradually lowering the price over time

Table 1.3 Pricing strategies

Pricing strategy	Target market	Pricing tactic	Advantages	Disadvantages
Competitive pricing	New and existing customers	• Setting a price that is similar to that of a local competitor, e.g. supermarkets price-matching goods sold by their competitors	• Because all businesses are charging the same price, it could damage the business's ability to compete • May attract new customers as the price is the same as their usual retailer	• Profit margins are likely to be low as the selling price may only be sufficient to cover the production costs of the goods • Businesses need to be creative in their methods of attracting customers as price alone will not encourage customers to the store
Price skimming	New customers	• Introduce the product at a high price and then gradually lower it over time, e.g. when Dyson introduced a bag-less cleaner there were no similar alternative products, so they could charge very high prices	• High prices can give a product a good image • A good image can lead customers to think the product is of very high quality • Businesses will make higher profits while the price is high, and this additional money helps pay back research costs that have been incurred	• Some customers will be lost due to the high price • Sales can be lost, reducing revenue as customers are put off by the higher price • There is a possibility that competitors will bring out lower priced products and therefore sales will be lost

Pricing strategy	Target market	Pricing tactic	Advantages	Disadvantages
Psychological pricing	New and existing customers	● Setting a price that appears attractive to a customer, e.g. selling a holiday for £999 rather than £1 000	● Attracts customers as it is perceived to be a good deal; this may increase customer numbers, revenue and profit margins ● Products are being sold for only slightly less than their true value	● Customers are becoming increasingly aware of this type of pricing and may be less susceptible than in the past ● Difficult to offer percentage discounts – it is difficult to offer 10% off 99p
Price penetration	New customers	● Introduce the product at a lower price than usual to attract customers. Gradually increase the price over time, e.g. new flavour crisps might be sold at half the price they will be sold at eventually	● Attracts customers to a product and encourages them try it in the hope they will continue to purchase it once prices increase. ● Price penetration is effective in increasing market share quickly	● While selling at the lower cost, revenue is lost and therefore profit is lower ● Products that have a very short life span, for example, fashion clothing, are not suited to this method of pricing because by the time the price rises, the product will no longer be in fashion

Activity

Fresh Food is a small supermarket based in the West of England. The company is introducing a new range of salads.

1 Analyse the advantages and disadvantages of the different pricing strategies that Fresh Food could use when introducing their new range of salads.

2 Recommend which pricing strategy Fresh Food should use when launching the new range of salads.

Key terms

Psychological pricing
Setting a price that appears attractive to a customer

Price penetration
Introducing a product at a lower price than usual to attract customers, then gradually increasing the price over time

4.3 Types of advertising methods used to attract and retain customers and their appropriateness

A wide range of advertising is available. Businesses must ensure that their advertising is focused on their target audience and appropriate to the products they are trying to sell.

Leaflets

Leaflets tend to be used by small businesses, as they are low cost and can be targeted to customers in the local area. For example, fast food take-away shops often use leaflets to promote their new menus.

Benefits
● Leaflets are relatively cheap to produce and can contain a large amount of information.
● They can be targeted to customers in the local area.
● They can be distributed to a wide range of potential customers.
● Leaflets are easy to read and have a good visual impact.

was £1000, now £999

Great summer sale

7 days in Spain including flights and villa

Figure 1.21 Psychological pricing

Disadvantages

- Leaflets are often thrown away once read, especially if they are of poor quality.
- Leaflets can be viewed as junk mail and thrown away without being read.
- As leaflets are not usually kept for a long period of time, they do not have a long-term impact.

Social media

The use of use social media such as Facebook and Twitter to advertise products and gather feedback is a rapidly growing area for many businesses.

Benefits

- Adverts on social media are relatively cheap to produce and distribute.
- Social media accounts can be used to update customers on current offers, new products and promotions.
- Social media allow access to international markets.
- Social media enable customers to provide feedback.

Disadvantages

- Social media are less useful when targeting an older market who are less 'tech savvy' and less likely to go online or use apps.
- Social media requires daily monitoring to prevent inappropriate comments being left.
- Social media increase the risk of negative reviews, information leaks or hacking of company or customer data.

Figure 1.22 Online advertisement

Websites

The use of websites to advertise products is a rapidly growing area for many businesses. Many businesses also have their own websites. A business can choose to:

- place adverts on search engine results pages
- pay for pop-ups (small internet browser windows that appear over the top of web pages used to attract attention)
- place adverts on social networking sites.

Benefits

- Adverts on websites are relatively cheap to produce and distribute.
- Websites can be used to update customers on current offers, new products and promotions.
- They have been proved to increase sales.
- Websites allow access to international markets.
- Websites enable customers to provide feedback.

Disadvantages
- Websites are less useful when targeting an older market who are less 'tech savvy' and less likely to go online or use apps.
- Websites increase the risk of negative reviews, information leaks or hacking of company or customer data.

Newspapers

It is estimated that about one-quarter of all expenditure on advertising in the UK is on newspaper adverts.

Businesses need to decide whether they want to advertise in national, local or free newspapers. Free and local newspaper advertisements are relatively cheap, whereas, large adverts in national newspapers are extremely expensive. Small businesses tend to focus on free and local newspapers to keep costs down and to target the customers that are most likely to purchase their products.

Figure 1.23 Newspaper advertisement

Benefits
- Costs of advertising in free and local newspapers are low.
- Local newspaper advertising can target local customers, directing them to specific local outlets.
- National newspapers are more widely read than local newspapers.
- National newspapers will have a broader reach.
- This method is effective in targeting older people who often read newspapers on a daily basis.

Disadvantages
- Advertising in national newspapers is very expensive.
- Unless the advert is in prime position, there may be competition for the reader's attention.
- Newspaper adverts are not targeted.
- Less effective when targeting younger people as they are less likely to read newspapers.

Magazines

Magazines are usually issued on a weekly or monthly basis and are aimed at a specific target market. While magazine advertisements will generally be more expensive than those in a newspaper, it is likely that the information will reach the customers that a business is trying to target. In addition, magazines tend to be kept longer than a newspaper and may also be shared with others.

Benefits
- Advertisements in magazines are targeted at a particular audience. Specific magazines target specific groups and therefore advertisements can be placed accordingly.
- Unlike leaflets, people tend to keep magazines.
- People often pass magazines they have purchased and read onto their family or friends.

Disadvantages

- Deadlines for advertisements may be months in advance. Good business planning is required to ensure adverts are placed in time to appear perhaps several months later, especially if they are part of a wider promotional campaign.
- Depending on the type of magazine chosen, advertising costs can be very expensive.
- Magazines often contain a vast number of advertisements, so there is a risk that a business's advertisement will be 'lost'.

Radio

Radio advertising can be used to reach a particular target market. For example, a sportswear store may choose to advertise during breaks in a football show on their local radio station.

Benefits

- Speech and music can attract attention to a radio advertisement.
- Specific audiences can be targeted by choosing an appropriate station and programme on which to advertise.
- Radio advertisements can be produced relatively quickly.

Disadvantages

- Radios are often used as background noise, so the advertisement may be missed or ignored.
- Prime slots in the morning or evening when people are driving to and from work will be considerably more expensive than other times during the day.
- There is no way of saving the advertisement – the listener needs to take all of the information in at once.

Activity

Claret Gym, in Turf Town, has been open for two months. The gym is independently owned and is not part of a national chain. There are several other larger gyms in the area but the exceptional customer service offered by Claret Gym has acted as its unique selling point when first attracting customers.

Advise the owners of Claret Gym the most appropriate advertising methods to attract and retain members.

For planning purposes, you could use the table below.

Advertising method	Description	Advantages	Disadvantages

4.4 Sales promotion techniques to attract and retain customers and the appropriateness of each

Sales promotions are used by organisations to provide a short-term boost to their sales (Figure 1.24). There are number of different techniques that can be used, as shown in Figure 1.25.

Figure 1.24 Sales display

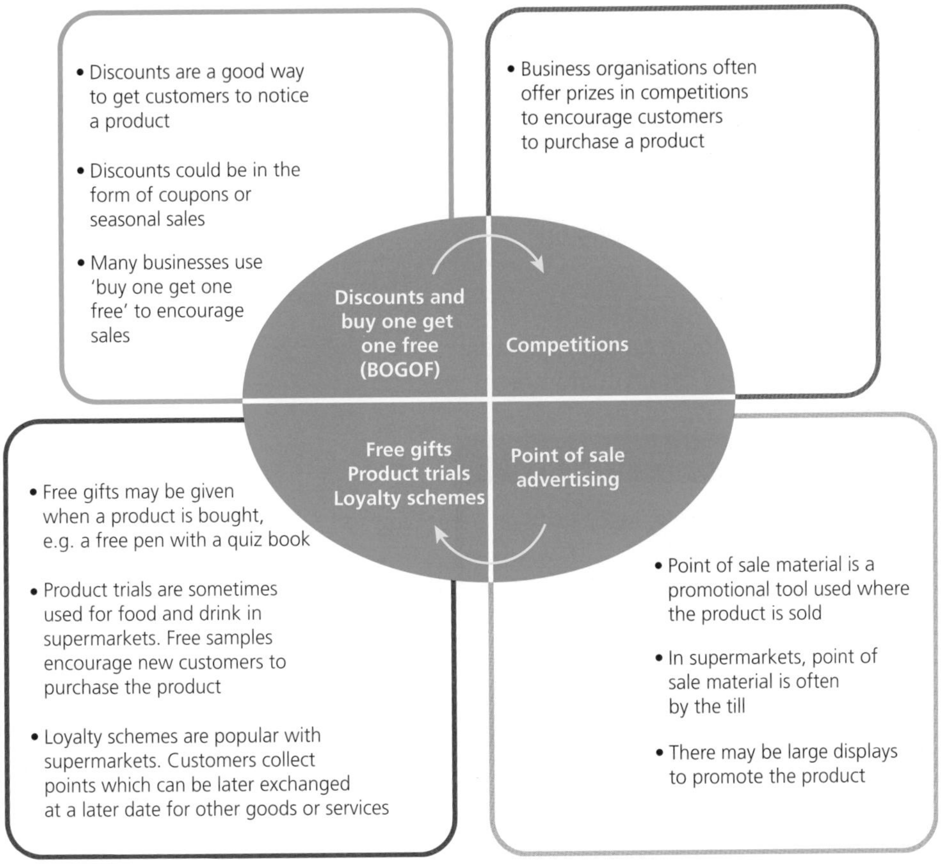

- Discounts are a good way to get customers to notice a product

- Discounts could be in the form of coupons or seasonal sales

- Many businesses use 'buy one get one free' to encourage sales

- Business organisations often offer prizes in competitions to encourage customers to purchase a product

Discounts and buy one get one free (BOGOF)

Competitions

Free gifts Product trials Loyalty schemes

Point of sale advertising

- Free gifts may be given when a product is bought, e.g. a free pen with a quiz book

- Product trials are sometimes used for food and drink in supermarkets. Free samples encourage new customers to purchase the product

- Loyalty schemes are popular with supermarkets. Customers collect points which can be later exchanged at a later date for other goods or services

- Point of sale material is a promotional tool used where the product is sold

- In supermarkets, point of sale material is often by the till

- There may be large displays to promote the product

Figure 1.25 Sales promotion techniques

Activity

Advise the owners of Claret Gym (see page 42) on the most appropriate sales promotion techniques that could be used to attract and retain members. For planning purposes, you could use the table below.

Sales promotion technique	Description	Advantages	Disadvantages

(see page 42)

Stretch activity

1 Carry out internet research to review the benefits of loyalty schemes offered by three different supermarkets.

2 Prepare a table that compares and contrasts the different features of each loyalty scheme.

3 Write a paragraph to explain which supermarket's loyalty schemes most attracts you as a customer.

4.5 How customer service is used to attract and retain customers

Customer service is the way in which a business looks after its customers.

Customer engagement, product knowledge and after sales service

Excellent customer service will ensure that a business attracts new customers and retains its existing ones. In order to provide excellent customer service, employees need:

- good communication skills
- patience to understand the customers' needs and wants
- attention to detail – it is important that employees focus on customer requirements
- good product knowledge
- excellent personal presentation – employees should be appropriately dressed and act in a manner that will attract and retain customers.

Activity

In pairs, think about a time where you have experienced poor customer service when out shopping.

1 What made the experience poor and how did this make you feel about buying from that business?

2 Discuss how you think the customer service experience could have been improved.

Customer engagement

Each stakeholder group will have their own particular interest in a business organisation. By engaging with these stakeholder groups, business organisations will aim to benefit from their skills and abilities. Business organisations may engage with customers online via their websites, social media accounts as well as in person within shops and stores.

For example, by engaging with customers the business organisation will increase its reputation. This provides the business organisation with the opportunity to increase their sales and ultimately their profit levels.

Engaging with customers also involves gaining customer feedback. This is very important to business organisations. Without having a clear understanding of what customers need and want, a new business organisation is unlikely to succeed. Business organisations have to make a decision about how to receive feedback from their customers.

Product knowledge

Customer service advisers are required to have an in-depth knowledge of the products and services they are selling. Without appropriate subject knowledge, customers may be given incorrect information or may decide to purchase their goods from another supplier.

After sales service

After sales service is part of the customer service offered to customers. It is the way in which a business organisation looks after its customers once a purchase has been made.

Excellent customer service will ensure that a business organisation attracts new customers and retains its existing ones. In order to provide excellent customer service, employees will need different attributes; for example, good communication skills, patience, attention to detail etc.

Many organisations treat their staff as their most valuable asset. Employees that have excellent product knowledge and who are able to engage with customers about the business's products and services are likely to attract and retain customers.

Businesses understand that to offer excellent customer service, it is not enough for staff to engage with customers before and during a sale – they need to offer an excellent after-sales services too.

Most organisations now employ telephone customer service assistants who are able to deal with exchanges, queries about deliveries and damaged products as well as offer advice on how to use a product. Customer service employees need to enjoy dealing with the public and be friendly and helpful at all times.

Activity

Over the last 20 years, the cruise industry has grown in popularity and there are now a large number of cruise specialists offering this type of holiday.

In order to differentiate themselves from other travel agents, cruise specialists offer excellent customer service. The staff are usually experienced cruise passengers themselves, so they can offer excellent product information and are frequently available seven days a week to offer advice to passengers before they travel as well as during the cruise and on their return.

Identify and explain three factors that the cruise specialists need to consider when using customer service to attract and retain customers.

Test your knowledge

1 Explain how the selling price of a product is decided.
2 Define the term competitive pricing.
3 Identify and describe three advertising methods that could be used by a clothing retailer.
4 Identify and describe three sales promotion techniques for a new fast food restaurant opening in a local town.
5 Explain why customer service is important to a small business organisation.

LO5 Understand factors for consideration when starting up a business

This learning outcome covers important factors that need to be considered when setting up a new business. You will review the different forms of business ownership, how these can be financed and why a business plan is vital when setting up a new business.

Teaching content

In this learning outcome you will cover:

5.1 Appropriate forms of ownership for business start-ups

5.2 Sources of capital for business start-ups

5.3 The importance of a business plan

5.1 Appropriate forms of ownership for business start-ups

The different forms of ownership for business start-ups, as well as their advantages and disadvantages, are outlined in Table 1.4 below.

Getting started

In pairs, discuss the possible benefits and potential problems of an individual currently working on their own taking on a partner to work with them.

🔑 **Key terms**

Sole trader A business that is owned and controlled by one person

Unlimited liability The business owner(s) are personally liable for the debts of the business in the event that the business cannot pay them

Table 1.4 Types of business ownership

Type of ownership	Definition	Examples	Advantages	Disadvantages
Sole trader	A business owned and controlled by one individual	● Plumber ● Electrician ● Mobile hairdresser working alone	● Easy to set up ● Low set-up costs ● The owner makes all of the business decisions, reducing the time taken to make a decision ● Sole traders can choose their own working hours, holidays, etc. ● Limited legal requirements in relation to accounting, etc.	● Difficult for the business to grow very large due to the amount of money available to the sole trader ● Banks are less keen to lend to sole traders as they view them as more of a risk ● Difficult for the business to grow as there is a limit to the amount of work one person can do on their own ● The sole trader has no one to share responsibility or decisions with ● The sole trader may have to work long hours and will not be paid during time off for a holiday or illness ● A sole trader has **unlimited liability**, which means their personal assets such as their house or car could be sold to meet the debts of the business if they could not be paid

→

→

Type of ownership	Definition	Examples	Advantages	Disadvantages
Partnership (see also section on Limited liability partnerships below)	A partnership is a business that is owned and controlled by two or more individuals. In most cases, there are 2–20 partners. However, this number can be exceeded for professional partnerships, e.g. accountants and solicitors	● Estate agents ● Accountants ● Solicitors ● Small/ medium sized retail stores	● Greater capital investment available from the different partners ● Partners bring different skills and attributes to aid the business ● Responsibility and risk are shared among the partners ● Partners can discuss queries before finalising decisions ● Increased public image compared to sole traders	● Decision making can be time consuming, as all partners need to be consulted ● There is a potential for disagreement and conflict in decision making ● All partners are jointly responsible for the business debt – like sole traders, a partnership has unlimited liability. (All partners would need to pay the business's debts if they could not be paid)
Franchise	A franchise is a business organisation where the franchisor (the owner of the business idea) grants a licence (the franchise) to another business (the franchisee), so they can sell their brand or business idea. The franchisor owns the business idea and decides how the business will be operated and run	● McDonalds ● Pizza Hut ● Starbucks	● Limited business and industry experience are required, as the business model already exists ● The franchisee still owns the business but not the idea ● As the franchise will be well known, it is easier to raise finance ● The franchisee benefits from the skills, advice and support of the franchisor ● It is easier to gain customers, as the brand is already well known and recognised	● The initial and on-going costs of operating a franchise are not cheap ● The franchisee will need to stick to the marketing activities agreed by the franchisor ● May be difficult to break into a new area if competing with other franchisees

Limited liability partnerships

In a limited liability partnership, each partner of the business is not personally liable for the business's debts if they cannot be paid. A partner is only liable to the amount of money he or she invested into the business – this is known as **limited liability**.

 Key terms

Franchise A business where the franchisor (the owner of the business idea) grants a licence (the franchise) to another business (the franchisee) to operate their brand or business idea

Partnership A business that is owned and controlled by two or more individuals

Limited liability The business owners are only liable for the debts of a business up to the amount of money they have invested in the business

Table 1.5 Features of each form of business ownership

	Owners	Basic legal requirements to start the business	Liability?	Responsibility for decision making	Distribution of profit to the owners
Sole trader	One business owner	● The sole trader will register with HMRC to pay taxation on profits made	Unlimited	Single owner	Single owner
Partnership (unlimited liability)	Two or more business owners	● Each partner will register with HMRC to pay taxation on their share of the profits ● A partnership agreement may be drawn up to identify the key role and responsibilities of each partner. This will include how profits/loss are shared	Unlimited	All partners equally unless there is a partnership agreement that states differently	All partners equally unless there is a partnership agreement that states differently
Limited liability partnerships	Two or more business owners	● Each partner will register with HMRC to pay taxation on their share of the profits made ● A partnership agreement may be drawn up to identify the key role and responsibilities of each partner. This may include how profits/loss are shared	Limited	All partners equally unless there is a partnership agreement that states differently	All partners equally unless there is a partnership agreement that states differently
Franchise	The franchisor owns the business idea. The franchisee will own the right to use the business idea and the individual business that is set up	● The franchisee will register with HMRC to pay taxation on profits made ● The franchisee will need to pay the agreed amount of money to the franchisor each year	Varies depending on the franchise	The franchisor is responsible for overall decisions relating to the business design and idea, e.g. store layout and brand logos The franchisee will decide on working hours, holidays, etc.	The franchisee will earn the profit from the franchise but will need to pay an annual fee and agreed percentage of the profit to the franchisor
Private limited company	Shareholders (family and friends)	Documents need to be submitted to Companies House – **Memorandum and Articles of Association**.	Limited	Directors appointed by the shareholders to run the company on their behalf.	Via dividends
Public limited company	Shareholders (the general public)	Documents need to be submitted to Companies House – Memorandum and Articles of Association.	Limited	Directors appointed by the shareholders to run the company on their behalf.	Via dividends

When limited companies are set up there are a number of legal requirements that they have to follow. These include the need to submit the company's Memorandum of Association and Articles of Association to Companies House. In addition, the company needs to register with HMRC to pay tax on any profits made by the company. For limited companies, the responsibility for decision making may not belong to the owners or shareholders. The company owners/shareholders may employ directors or other individuals to make decisions for the company on their behalf.

Key terms

Memorandum of Association
Details of the nature, purpose and structure of the company

Articles of Association
Details of the internal rules of the company

Activity

Barry is planning to open a bakery business selling sandwiches, pies and cakes to local businesses. He is unsure of what type of business structure to choose.

Prepare a short report offering Barry advice on his potential options.

 Case study

Lea is a self-employed painter and decorator. She has been in business for 15 years and has established a number of loyal customers. To improve the efficiency of her business, Lea is considering forming a partnership with her friends Olson, who is a self-employed interior designer.

Question

Discuss the potential benefits and drawbacks of Lea and Olson forming a partnership.

5.2 Sources of capital for business start-ups

When starting and setting up a new business, it is vital that the owner is able to secure the capital (also referred to as finance or money) required to fund the business. This capital is often used to pay for premises, equipment, machinery and advertising. Once set up, a business will need further finance to operate on a day-to-day basis.

After a period of time, the business may decide to expand. It may need to purchase additional machinery, rent larger premises or pay extra staff. However, it is very unlikely it will have made sufficient profits to do this without additional funding from outside the business.

As the business grows and expands, there is the possibility that some customers will not pay their debts immediately, leading to a short fall in available cash. The business will therefore need short-term capital to pay staff wages, to settle debts and to purchase stock to sell.

There are a number of ways a business can source the capital that it requires, as shown in Figure 1.26.

Figure 1.26 Start-up finance

Personal savings

Personal savings is money that the owner has invested into their business. It is usually long-term finance and will come from their savings. There is no cost for this type of finance, other than the loss of interest that could have been earned if the money had remained in a bank account. If the business fails, the owner will not get their savings back.

The benefit of this method of finance is that is does not have to be repaid and no interest will be due. However, there may be a limit to the amount of money that the owner can invest.

Friends and family

Friends and family are often willing to lend owners money to start up their business. As with personal savings, this type of capital is often lent without any charges or fees and is often only repaid once the business has become successful. If the business fails, friends and families will not get their money back, so this type of lending is high risk.

The benefit of this type of capital is that it may not have to be repaid and no interest will be due. However, there is a limit to the amount of money that friends and family will be willing and able to invest.

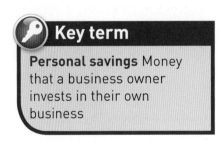

Key term

Personal savings Money that a business owner invests in their own business

Loans

Loans are usually a longer-term source of finance and are offered by banks, building societies or other financial institutions. The lender will ask to see evidence that the business can repay the amount in full. Loans are usually repaid over a period of three to ten years.

In return for lending the money, the lender will charge interest. This will need to be repaid along with the amount of money borrowed. In a number of cases, the business will be asked to provide security (also known as collateral) in case the business cannot repay the debt. This might include assets such as manufacturing equipment or even a building such as the owner's home. If the business fails and is unable to repay the loan, the lender may then take possession of the assets put up as security.

One advantage of a loan is that set repayments spread the cost of the loan over a period of time which enables the business to budget for them. The disadvantages of a loan are that high interest payments can make it expensive and the lender may require security for the loan.

Key terms

Loan Long-term source of finance offered by banks, building societies or other financial institutions

Crowdfunding Groups of investors that join together to offer funding to a business

Figure 1.27 A business owner may speak to a bank to obtain finance

Crowdfunding

This is a fast-growing and relatively new method of finance for new businesses. Instead of one person investing in a business idea and taking ownership of a large part of the business, **crowdfunding** asks a group or 'crowd' of investors for funding. For example, if a new business required £100 000, instead of one person investing that sum there could be 100 investors all willing to invest £1 000. This shares the risk of investment should the business fail.

The benefit of crowdfunding is that there is a higher probability of raising the funds than asking one individual for the money. A drawback is the business owner may have to give a proportion of their business to the investors. A further drawback is that if the crowdfunding target is not reached, any money already pledged by investors is usually returned, meaning the business will receive nothing.

Small business grants

Business start-up grants may be available from banks, various charities or the government. There are usually set criteria that need to be met in order to access the grants. For example, some grants are available only for those under 25 or they may be offered in areas of the country where there are high levels of unemployment.

When applying for a **small business grant**, the business owner will need to have a clear business plan and a model of how their business will operate and progress in the future. (For more on business plans, see Unit R064, Section 5.3.)

One important advantage of a small business grant is that it does not have to be repaid. However, strict conditions are likely to apply and not every business will be eligible.

Business angels

A **business angel** is a wealthy entrepreneur who provides a business owner with a substantial sum of money to help them set up their business. In return, the owner agrees to give the business angel a proportion of the business's profits. The business angel is therefore taking a considerable personal risk by investing in the new business. However, if the business is successful, the business angel will receive a sizeable return on their investment.

Business angels provide a business owner with a large of amount of money to invest in their business and they may also offer advice and support in running the business. However, the business owner will usually have to give a proportion of their business to the business angel. The television programme, *Dragons' Den*, features small business owners pitching their ideas to business angels known as 'Dragons', in the hope they will invest in their business.

The appropriateness of each source of finance will depend on the following factors:

- Purpose – what does the business require the money for?
- Time period – how long does the business need the money for?
- Amount – how much money is required?
- Types of business – the size and type of ownership of the business will affect the finance that is available. For example, grants may only be able to organisations of a certain size.

Key terms

Small business grants Sums of money available from various charities or the government to help individuals set up a business

Business angel Wealthy entrepreneur who provides a business owner with a substantial sum of money to help set up a business; in return they receive a proportion of the business's profits

Figure 1.28 Business owners may pitch their ideas to business angels in order to obtain investment

Activity

Copy and complete the table to review the various sources of finance.

Source of capital	Description	Benefits	Problems
Own savings			
Friends and family			
Loans			
Crowdfunding			
Small business grants			
Business angels			

5.3 The importance of a business plan

A business plan is a document that describes a business's:

- objectives
- strategies
- market
- financial position and forecasts.

Why a business plan is needed

There are four main reasons why a business needs to prepare a **business plan**, as shown in Figure 1.29.

Key term

Business plan Description of a business's aims and targets. It summarises the actions required in order to make these a reality

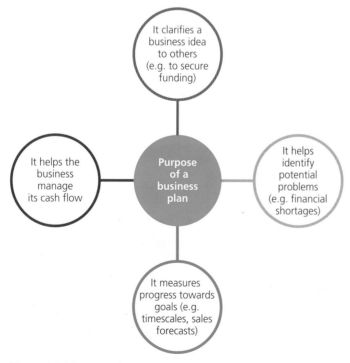

Figure 1.29 Reasons for preparing a business plan

The importance of managing cash flow

If a business runs out of cash, it will not be able to pay for its inventory (stock) or pay its workers. If this happens, a business is classed as insolvent. The owners will have to raise additional money or cease trading and close down the business.

To prevent this from happening, a business will carefully monitor its cash flow (on a weekly or monthly basis) to ensure it has sufficient money to pay its liabilities (debts it owes). The business will often plan ahead by preparing a cash flow forecast (see Unit R064, Section 6.2) to identify if additional finance is required.

What a business plan should detail

Simple business plans for internal use are usually prepared by the business owner or individual planning on setting up the business (the **entrepreneur**).

The content will vary depending on the type of business, but a business plan usually includes the following:

- A simple **description** of the business or business idea.
- **Business aims** – the goals the business would like to achieve.
- **Key business objectives** – a detailed picture of the steps the business needs to take in order to achieve its aims.
- **Key targets for the business** – a way of turning key objectives into goals that need to be met.
- **Business strategies** – long-term plans of action to achieve the goals and objectives.
- **Plans and forecasts** to demonstrate how the business will operate, including:
  - sales plan – number of sales expected over a stated period of time
  - marketing plan – how the business will market and advertise its products and services
  - financial forecast – for example, break-even analysis, profit forecasts.

Key term

Entrepreneur Individual who has a business idea and plans to set up a new business

Test your knowledge

1 Define the term franchise.
2 Explain the difference between a sole trader and a partnership.
3 Explain what is meant by 'unlimited liability'.
4 Identify and describe three sources of capital for a new business.
5 Discuss why a business may prepare a business plan.

Stretch activity

1 Use the internet to research and download a business plan template.
2 Working in small groups, decide on a business idea that you would like to develop. Complete the business plan template for your business idea.

LO6 Understand different functional activities needed to support a business start-up

This learning outcome identifies and reviews the different departments and functional areas of a business. You will gain an overview of what each functional area does within a business.

Teaching content

In this learning outcome you will cover:

6.1 The purpose of each of the main functional activities that may be needed in a new business

6.2 The main activities of each functional area

Getting started

Think about your school or college. Identify all of the different areas in the school that exist to ensure the school provides pupils with a good quality education. For example, the human resources department recruits teachers.

6.1 The purpose of each of the main functional activities that may be needed in a new business

There are four main **functional areas** that need to be considered when starting a new business, as shown in Figure 1.30

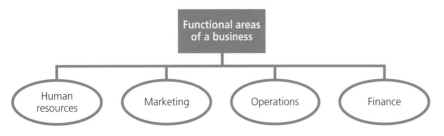

Figure 1.30 An organisation chart shows the functional areas of a business

Key term

Functional area A department that plays a specific role within an organisation and whose employees carry out a particular aspect of the work of the organisation. For example, in the finance area, the employees will all have skills in accounting

Small businesses, including many sole trader businesses, often do not have different departments for each of these functions. Instead, one person will carry out all of these activities. Although this reduces costs and may meet the needs of the business, it is unlikely that one individual will be skilled in each of these areas. He or she may have a general overview of knowledge but lack a detailed understanding of the different areas.

Human resources

It is often said that an organisation's human resources – its employees – is its most important asset. The human resources (HR) department is responsible for looking after all employees from recruitment to departure from the organisation, whether this is through retirement, redundancy or because they have a new job elsewhere. The HR department is responsible for all aspects of managing individuals who work within a business, for example, HR staff will:

- plan how many staff may be needed in the future, often referred to as 'manpower planning'
- prepare all the paperwork for a job vacancy – adverts, job descriptions, person specifications
- determine wages and salaries
- recruit and select employees
- provide training and development for all employees
- be responsible for employee welfare and motivation
- deal with employee complaints or grievances
- implement organisational policies, for example, health and safety
- deal with dismissals and redundancies.

Marketing

The marketing department promotes or advertises the organisation's products and services. The aim is to target customers and ensure they are fully aware of what the organisation offers. The marketing department therefore works to develop an understanding of the needs and wants of the organisation's customers, and is responsible for promotional activities that help to generate sales and business growth.

Operations

The operations department deals with the production processes within a business. It is responsible for overseeing, designing and controlling how production processes work. For example, in manufacturing businesses, the operations department looks after the maintenance of equipment and production lines. In this way, the operations department transforms business inputs, such as raw materials, into outputs that can be sold.

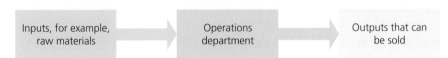

Inputs, for example, raw materials → Operations department → Outputs that can be sold

Figure 1.31 Operations department processes

Finance

The finance department of a business controls all monetary aspects of its operation. In particular, the finance department will consider how financial resources are allocated to different departments and ensure there is sufficient cash within the business to pay all of its bills. At various points in the year, the finance department will report on the financial position and performance of the organisation.

Activity

Lynne has secured a job as a barista (preparing and serving coffee) at a new coffee shop.

Discuss how each of the different functional areas of the coffee shop may affect Lynne.

Activity

1 In small groups, discuss which of these functional activities is most important to a business in its first year of trading.

2 Consider whether your response would change if you were discussing a business that had been in operation for 5 years.

6.2 The main activities of each functional area

Each of the functional areas described above has a number of key activities it must complete. No one area can work in isolation, so there needs to be good communication between the different functional areas, to ensure the organisation can operate successfully.

Human resources

The human resources area is responsible for the following activities:

- **Recruitment and selection of employees** – for example, advertising job vacancies, shortlisting candidates and interviewing and selecting the most appropriate candidate for the job.

- **Training and development of employees** – all employees are entitled to training while employed. For example, new employees receive induction training to familiarise them with the organisation and their job role. During their time with the organisation, they may receive a range of other training to ensure they have the skills required to perform their job.

- **Performance management of employees** – throughout the year, a business will review the performance of its employees. In some organisations, an employee's performance determines the amount of money they are paid.

- **Responsibility for health and safety in the workplace** – the human resources department is responsible for ensuring that all employees are safe at work. For example, employees will be trained in how to operate machinery and made aware of what to do in the event of a fire.

- **Ensuring compliance with employment legislation** – the human resources department will review all current employment legislation. This includes such things as working time directives, which state how long an employee can work during one day and how many breaks they need to take.

Marketing

The marketing department is responsible for researching the market in which the business operates and finding out what customers want (as discussed earlier in this unit, in Learning Outcome 1; see pages 3–17).

The marketing department is responsible for developing the business's marketing mix for a product or service. The marketing mix refers to the 4 Ps of marketing – price, product, place and promotion – which are used together to market a product or service (see Figure 1.32). The marketing mix affects the type of marketing undertaken by the business. For example, when marketing a product or service, no single element of the marketing mix is more important than another – they all link together. For example, a poor product is unlikely to sell even if it is priced at a very low price. A business needs to ensure that its products are appropriately priced, promoted and placed in a suitable position in the market.

Figure 1.32 The 4 Ps of the marketing mix

Operations

The operations area of a business is responsible for managing production processes. It will consider how the production processes are planned and how the products and services are to be produced.

Production planning

Any business organisation needs to carefully plan their production processes. This will involve working out how many products need to be produced and by when. Once this is known, the business organisation will decide on the most efficient use of their resources, (machinery, staff etc.) to meet these requirements.

Lean production

Lean production is a management approach that aims to cut waste. At the same time, the business focuses on high quality. The idea is used throughout the business organisation from design to distribution.

There are different methods of lean production. These include using cell production to produce goods and also benchmarking.

Producing the product or service

Business organisations tend to use one of four different production methods shown in Table 1.6 on the next page.

Table 1.6 Different production methods

Production Type	Description	Examples
One-off production/job production	One product is made at a time. Every product will be slightly different and usually made by hand and/or machine. The products will be expensive and very time consuming to make.	Painting Handmade jumper Bespoke jewellery
Batch production	Small quantities of identical products are made. This method also uses machinery and manpower. The products tend to be relatively expensive due to the labour costs. Every batch will be slightly different.	Coloured paint Knitting wool
Mass production	Usually completed on a production line and involves the assembly of different components or items. It is usually completed by machine and relatively cheap to operate.	Cars T-shirts Motorised parts
Continuous flow	This is similar to mass production except that in continuous flow operations, the production line is operated 24 hours a day, 7 days a week. This reduces the costs of stopping and starting production. Very few workers are required and the majority of the work is completed by machine.	Production of canned baked beans Mass produced loaves of bread

Figure 1.33 Continuous flow production

> ## Activity
>
> Working in pairs, write a list of different businesses in your local area.
>
> Decide which of the four different production methods outlined in Table 1.6 is used by each of the businesses you have identified.

Cell production

This production process:

- divides the production process into a series of stages
- is arranged around teams
- ensures each team completes a full unit of production instead of individuals completing one task
- allows each team to have responsibility for their work and see end results
- increases motivation
- increases responsibility
- improves quality.

Finished product   Finished product   Finished product

Figure 1.34 Cell production

Quality control

Quality control is an important aspect of any business. This is when a business will check that their products and services meet the required standards, so that customers will be satisfied when they purchase the product or service. For example, imagine if you purchased your favourite chocolate bar, and it did not taste the same as it normally does, or contained nuts when it didn't normally. Either of these situations would demonstrate that the quality control processes were not correct from the manufacturer. It is important therefore that the business informs potential investors what they will be doing to ensure that the standards of quality are high for the business.

Kaizen

Kaizen is a Japanese concept that focuses on gradual and continuous improvement. The idea is a whole-business philosophy. To ensure its success it is therefore important that everyone in the organisation buys into the concept and vision.

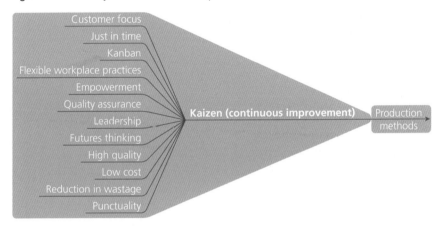

Figure 1.35 The Kaizen concept

Benchmarking

This is the continuous, systematic search for and implementation of best practice which leads to superior performance. The use of benchmarking will help a business to maintain and improve quality. Business organisations that benchmark will measure performance against others and aim to learn from the best firms in the world.

Business organisations will use benchmarking to assess the:

- reliability of products
- ability to deliver items on time
- ability to send out correct invoices
- time taken to produce a product

Quality assurance

Most business organisations will have a quality assurance system where they will maintain a certain level of quality for every product or service that they produce and sell. This usually means that they will focus on every stage of the production and delivery processes.

Total quality management
A management approach which seeks to involve all employees in the process of improving quality.

Stock control
Just in time (JIT)
JIT means that stock arrives on the production line just as it is needed. This minimises the amount of stock that has to be stored (reducing storage costs).

JIT has many benefits and may appear an obvious way to organise production but it is a complicated process which requires efficient handling.

Table 1.7 Advantages and disadvantages of just in time (JIT)

Advantages	Disadvantages
Improves cash flow as stock is not tied up in stocks	Needs suppliers and employees to be reliable
Reduces waste – stock does not go out of date	May be difficult to manage with surges in demand
Less factory storage space is needed	Loss of reputation if orders are delivered late

Logistics
When business organisations grow, they are often not able to complete all of the business tasks themselves. They need to 'outsource' some of their operations. Outsourcing means that a business organisation will hire another business to do some of the work for them. For example, this may be payroll operations, IT operations or website design.

Small businesses, for example sole traders, also outsource various aspects of their business as they do not have all of the necessary skills available to do the work themselves.

The outsourced work is usually of high quality but is considerably more expensive than being completed in-house.

Finance

The finance department is responsible for all tasks concerned with money and will also analyse the financial reports that are prepared. The finance department:

- organises and allocates financial resources – for example, it ensures that sufficient money is given to the other departments, such as marketing and production, to enable them to carry out their role
- reports on financial performance – it will prepare detailed reports assessing the organisation's profitability and liquidity, etc.
- monitors cash flow – as part of its analysis, the finance department prepares cash budgets or cash flow forecasts, in order to review the amount of money available to the business. Table 1.8 shows an example of a cash flow forecast.

Read about it

www.businesslink.co.uk – provides practical examples on how to be a successful business person.

www.socialenterprise.org.uk – a national body for social enterprise, the website provides excellent practical examples.

Table 1.8 Cash flow forecast

	January	February	March	April	May	June
	£	£	£	£	£	£
Income						
Sales	20000	30000	50000	75000	50000	30000
Total income	20000	30000	50000	75000	50000	30000
Expenditure						
Inventory	1000	3000	5000	0	3000	5000
Wages and salaries	10000	10000	10000	10000	10000	10000
Rent and rates	5000	5000	5000	5000	5000	5000
Total expenditure	16000	18000	20000	15000	18000	20000
Net cash flow	4000	12000	30000	60000	32000	10000
Opening Balance	20000	24000	36000	66000	126000	158000
Closing balance	24000	36000	66000	126000	158000	168000

Activity

In small groups, think about a car manufacturer producing cars on a production line.

Copy and complete the table below by describing how the car manufacturer uses the four functional areas listed.

Functional area	Purpose	Main activities
Human resources		
Marketing		
Operations		
Finance		

Stretch activity

Choose an organisation with which you are familiar.

1 Identify the key functional areas within the organisation.

2 List the main activities each functional area completes.

Test your knowledge

1 Define the term 'functional area'.

2 Discuss the purpose of the functional area of marketing.

3 Explain the role of the operations department.

4 Identify three key activities of the human resource department.

5 Explain the main activities of the finance department in an organisation.

Question practice

Part A: Multiple choice questions

1 Which of the following is an **internal** factor for a business?
   a Customer needs
   b Increased taxation rates
   c New government legislation
   d Staffing costs

Additional guidance

   a Customer needs are an external factor.
   b Increased taxation rates are an external factor.
   c New government legislation is an external factor.
   d **Correct answer** – staffing costs are an internal factor.

2 A business breaks even at the level of output where:
   a total profits = total costs
   b fixed costs = total revenue
   c total revenue = total costs
   d variable costs = total revenue

Additional guidance

   a Total profits are calculated at the end of a financial period by deducting costs from revenue.
   b Fixed costs are a component of total costs but do not equal total revenue.
   c **Correct answer** – a business breaks even when total revenue is equal to total costs.
   d Variable costs are a component of total costs but do not equal total revenue.

3 Which of the following is an **internal** influence when developing a new product?
   a Staffing issues
   b Economic issues
   c Legal issues
   d Technological issues

Additional guidance

   a **Correct answer** – staffing issues are an internal factor.
   b Economic issues are an external factor.
   c Legal issues are an external factor.
   d Technological development is an external factor.

4 Which of the following forms part of the marketing mix?
   a Cost
   b Advertising
   c Price
   d Resources

→

→

Additional guidance

a Cost is not part of the marketing mix.

b Employees are not part of the marketing mix.

c **Correct answer** – price is one of the four Ps (price, place, product, promotion) of the marketing mix.

d Resources are not part of the marketing mix.

5 Which of the following are used when completing desk research?

a Consumer trials

b Focus groups

c Individual observations

d Newspaper articles

Additional guidance

a Consumer trials are used for field research.

b Focus groups are used for field research.

c Individual observations are used for field research.

d **Correct answer** – newspaper articles are used for desk research.

6 Which of the following is **not** a functional area in an organisation?

a Finance

b Reception

c Human resources

d Marketing

Additional guidance

a Finance is a functional area of an organisation.

b **Correct answer** – the reception in an organisation is not a functional area.

c Human resources is a functional area of an organisation.

d Marketing is a functional area of an organisation.

7 Samantha uses a questionnaire to gather information for her café. What type of market research is Samantha using?

a Market segmentation

b Primary research

c Secondary research

d Desk research

Additional guidance

a Market segmentation involves splitting the market for a product or service into different groups (segments), for example, according to customers' age, gender or occupation.

b **Correct answer** – questionnaires are a form of primary research.

c Secondary research refers to information from internal data, books/newspapers/trade magazines, competitors' data, government publications and statistics and purchased research material, e.g. from Mintel.

d Desk research is another term for secondary research.

Question practice

Part B Short-answer questions

8 James owns and runs a butchers shop in the South West of England. The shop is now facing major competition from a large new supermarket that has located on the edge of the town.

   James is considering forming a partnership with his sister, Jacqueline, to try to compete with the supermarket.

   a) Identify and explain **two** advantages of James forming a partnership with his sister. [4 marks]

Mark scheme and additional guidance

Expected answers	Marks	Additional guidance
Advantages of forming a partnership may include: ● Easy to set up and change from a sole trader to a partnership **(1)**; there are no legal formalities as in the formation of a company **(1)** ● Shared responsibility **(1)** – James and his sister will share the business responsibilities **(1)** ● Specialisation **(1)** – James and his sister will have different specialisms which will help the business grow **(1)** ● Increased capital **(1)** – James and his sister can both invest in the business **(1)** ● Holiday/sickness cover **(1)** – James and his sister can cover for each other, so the business can continue to operate **(1)** ● Consultation **(1)** – James and his sister can discuss issues and consult with one another over business decisions **(1)**	4	Award one mark for an identified advantage and one mark for an explanation of the advantage.

Candidate answer

● A partnership is easy to set up.

● Jacqueline can help James with the work in the business, so he can go on holiday.

Marks awarded and rationale

● The first point is correct for one mark but has not been explained for the second mark.

● The second point is correct for one mark and has been explained for the second mark.

● Three out of a possible four marks awarded.

Question practice

b) Identify **three** promotional methods James could use to attract and retain his customers. [3 marks]

Mark scheme and additional guidance

Expected answers	Marks	Additional guidance
Sales promotion techniques include: ● discounts ● competitions ● buy-one-get-one-free (BOGOF) ● point-of-sale advertising ● free gifts ● product trials.	3	Award one mark for each method to a maximum of three marks.

Candidate answer

● Offer a discount to the customer.
● Provide a free gift.
● Put an advert in the newspaper.

Marks awarded and rationale

● The first two points are correct, but the third point is not a sales promotion technique.
● Two out of three marks awarded.

Question practice

c) James is considering using either the local newspaper or a local radio station to advertise his butchers shop to help him compete against the new supermarket.

Recommend which method of advertising you think James should use. Justify your answer. [8 marks]

Candidate answer

If James advertises in local newspapers, it will be low cost. James should be able to afford this, and it will widen his target audience. This is because many people read local newspapers.

James needs to remember that not everyone in his local area will read a newspaper so not all of his target audience will see his advertisement. If James uses repeat adverts in local papers, this could be expensive and would reduce his profits.

I would advise James to advertise in the local paper as this should provide the local community with information about his store and allow him to compete effectively with the supermarket.

Mark scheme and additional guidance

Expected answers	Marks	Additional guidance
Advertising in local newspapers Advantages: ● Cost of advertising in free and local newspapers is low ● Local newspaper advertising targets local customers ● This method is effective in targeting the older generation who often read newspapers on a daily basis Disadvantages: ● Local newspapers have a smaller readership compared to national newspapers ● Unless the advert is in a prime position, there may be competition for the reader's attention ● Newspaper adverts are not targeted ● This method is less effective when targeting the younger generation **Advertising on the local radio** Advantages: ● Use of sound and music can make a radio advertisement attract attention ● Specific audiences can be targeted by the radio advertisement by choosing an appropriate station and programme on which to advertise ● Radio advertisements can be produced very quickly ● Considerably cheaper than television adverting Disadvantages: ● Radios are often used as background noise, so the advertisement may be missed or ignored ● Prime slots in the morning or evening when people are driving to and from work will be considerably more expensive than other times during the day ● The listener cannot 'save' the content of the advert to refer to later – they need to take all of the information in at once	8	**1–2 marks** Candidate identifies benefits of one/both methods of advertising. **3–4 marks** Candidate explains one/both methods of advertising. **5–6 marks** Candidate analyses at least one method of advertising. **7–8 marks** Candidate evaluates more than one method, with a justified recommendation based on analysis of both methods of advertising.

Marks awarded and rationale

In this answer, the candidate has only talked about one of the two methods listed in the question. This means that they score a maximum of six marks out of a possible eight.

The learner has:

● identified a benefit of James using the local paper
● made an attempt to explain how the newspaper could be used to advertise his business
● analysed the local paper as a method of advertisement.

R065 Design a business proposal

About this unit

The aim of this unit is to design a product using a business challenge scenario. You will then produce a proposal that explains who your customers might be, identifies market research methods, states how you will advertise your product to your customers, calculates costs and then justifies your pricing strategies. Once completed, you will be able to determine whether this proposal is a realistic option. The business knowledge and skills you learn will enable you to complete this unit.

Learning outcomes

LO1 Be able to identify the customer profile for a business challenge

LO2 Be able to complete market research to aid decisions relating to the business challenge

LO3 Be able to develop a design proposal for a business challenge

LO4 Be able to review whether a business proposal is viable.

How will I be assessed?

This unit is assessed by an assignment that will be set by the OCR examination board. You will complete this assignment individually and in your lessons at school. Your teachers will mark the work using the mark scheme.

LO1 Be able to identify the customer profile for a business challenge

For this learning outcome, you will learn why it is important for a business to identify its potential customers and develop an understanding of their age, gender, occupation, income, interests and lifestyle. This is known a building a 'customer profile'.

Getting started

Look at the following descriptions of products and for each, decide which of the categories below the target customers would fit into.

- Sports app watch
- Extra-light walking poles
- Interactive video game featuring characters from a popular film
- Waterproof camera which can be used for deep-sea diving
- Combined greenhouse and shed

Sex	Male Female
Age	5–10 11–15 16–20 21–30 31–40 41–50 51+
Enjoys	Active sports Games consoles Holidays abroad New technology

Teaching content

In this learning outcome you will:

1.1 Identify potential customers and build a customer profile

1.1 Identify potential customers and build a customer profile

Identifying **potential customers** is important when considering a new business venture, as without customers to purchase its products, a business will not survive. Before starting a business, it is important to spend time researching what other businesses are producing that may be similar to your business idea. You will need to offer something different, so that people buy your product rather than those of your competitors.

 Key term

Potential customers People who are interested in the products or services that you sell and who may be persuaded to buy them

Market segmentation is when a specific market is divided into different customer groups to enable a business to target these customers according to their own specific needs and wants. One way to illustrate this is to think about toothpaste. Most people use toothpaste, but there are lots of different types available, with different features that appeal to different people. When choosing toothpaste, a customer will have to decide the following:

- preferred brand
- tube size
- features that are important to him or her, e.g. best for teeth whitening/fresh breath/sensitivity/suitable for children
- price.

Key term

Market segmentation
Dividing the market for a product or service into sections or segments in order to target particular types of customers

Benefits of market segmentation

Segmenting the market can benefit the business in several ways:

Increased future sales
Understanding the needs and wants of customers that purchase your product hopefully means they will continue to buy your products for many years – this is called 'repeat custom'. Loyal customers who provide repeat custom help to maintain and even increase sales. Today, loyal customers are hard for a business to achieve, as consumers are generally more demanding and want quality products at cheaper prices. If customers are dissatisfied, they can easily share this dissatisfaction with the business or friends via social media.

Greater knowledge of the market
By completing research into the segmentation of the business market, a business will have greater knowledge of the market it is potentially entering – and knowledge is power! The more knowledge a business has, the more it will be able to satisfy the needs of its customers by producing the products they want. Continued research will enable the business to fulfil these needs and wants throughout the life of the product.

Ability to target particular groups
Specific products are targeted to particular groups of consumers, as businesses cannot produce products that meet the needs of every consumer. Targeting specific groups means that a business can concentrate on producing products that will appeal to them. Advertising will be targeted at these potential customers, who will react to the advertising and then hopefully buy the product.

Prevent losses
If a business understands its customers, it can produce a product that will sell and make the business profitable. All businesses must avoid losing money, so producing products that meet specific customers' needs will help prevent losses and enable the business to be successful.

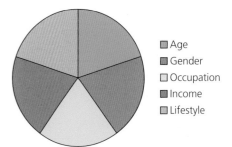

Figure 2.1 Market segmentation

Apply market segmentation

A market can be divided in several ways – some of the most common are by age, gender, occupation, income and lifestyle. Table 2.1 gives some examples of types of segmentation.

Table 2.1 Market segmentation

Segmentation	How segmentation is used	Examples of products that use this type of segmentation
Age	Products may be aimed at babies, toddlers, young children, pre-teens, teenagers, young adults, middle-aged adults and those of retirement age.	Disney Store sells toys, games and clothing that are suitable for babies, toddlers and young children. B&Q aim their products, such as paint, tools and gardening equipment, at adults of all ages.
Gender	Some products are aimed at females and some at males, while some products are aimed at both genders.	Make-up, fragrance and some types of vitamins are marketed to females. Haircare and skincare ranges for men are increasingly promoted to males. Radox is a range of shower gels for both males and females; they are targeted at different groups through scent, packaging and advertising.
Occupation	Products can be targeted at customers who may be employed in a specific job.	Pharmaceutical companies promote the latest medicines to doctors; builders' merchants offer professional ranges of tools and safety equipment to those working in the construction industry; cash-and-carry stores sell stock to small retail outlets such as corner shops.
Income	Products that attract a high price and which are considered a luxury item are targeted at customers with higher-than-average incomes; other businesses target customers on a budget.	Molten Brown produce toiletries that many consider to be a luxury product. Aldi and Lidl attract customers with a limited budget.
Lifestyle	People spend money on items related to hobbies and interests they enjoy doing in their spare time, for example, camping.	Go Outdoors specialise in products for people who enjoy outdoor activities, such as hiking boots, tents, sleeping bags.

Activity

Toothpaste is a product that we all use and there are many different types and brands available.

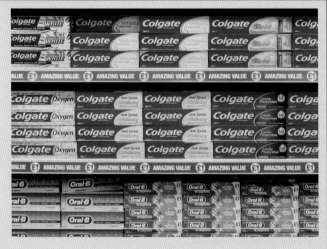

1 In pairs, answer the following questions:

   a Which toothpaste do you use?

   b Why do you use this particular one?

   c How long have you been using it?

   d Would you consider changing it? If yes, which one would you purchase and why? If not, why not?

   e What would persuade you to change your current toothpaste?

Feed back your answers to the class in a group discussion.

2 a Identify which segmentation of the market you consider your toothpaste brand to be within. Why do you think this is?

   b Think of the different types of toothpaste used in your class and decide which segment of the market each one falls into.

Activity

The market for coffee shops has enjoyed enormous growth in the past ten years. There is intense competition between the market leaders, Costa, Starbucks and Caffé Nero. The coffee and other hot and cold drinks they sell try to cater for all tastes.

Think about how many of these coffee shop outlets there are in your local area. These businesses have learnt that they need to target their products at certain segments of the market in order to ensure they gain repeat customers and continue being successful.

1 Copy the market segmentation chart shown in Figure 2.1 and then choose a selection of different products sold by the coffee shop outlet of your choice and place them into the segmentation chart according to the segments shown. Share your answers with the class.

2 Discuss your market segmentation chart with another member of the class. You should each explain and justify your reasons for placing the products chosen into the various segments.

Stretch activity

This task will focus on researching the types of coffee shops compared to the products that they sell. Research the different coffee shops in your local area; these probably range from high street retailers such as Starbucks to independent local coffee shops.

1 Write a paragraph to show your understanding of market segmentation.

2 Explain how each of the businesses you have researched might segment their target market, for example by having a childrens' play area to welcome and encourage families.

Customer profiling

Customer profiling is when a business uses knowledge of its customers and research into market segmentation to build up an image or profile of its likely customers. This information is used to build up a picture of the target customer for a particular product and might include details of where such a customer might live, their likely occupation and income level, how old they are and what they like to buy. The business then uses this customer profile to target its products at similar customers.

Figure 2.2 shows a man and woman running outside with a young child. We assume from this image that they are the parents of the young child. The child is probably under two years old and the parents are in their thirties. As they are running, the couple are

Figure 2.2 Customer profiling

assumed to have an interest in fitness and to enjoy being in the fresh air. If a business has a product that is aimed at people in their thirties, who have a family, who like fitness and being outdoors, then it is likely this product will appeal to the people shown in Figure 2.2. By establishing a likely set of characteristics for a target buyer, a business can identify a customer profile for its product or service.

Activity

Using your knowledge of market segmentation, work in groups to create a customer profile for the type of customer who might buy a new healthy cereal bar that has no added sugar, is suitable for vegetarians, is high in calcium and is an energy boost specifically for outdoor activities. The cereal bars will be priced at £4.99 for a box of five bars and only sold in health food shops.

Test your knowledge

1 Define market segmentation.
2 Why is segmenting the market helpful to a business? Explain your answer.
3 What are the benefits to a business of segmenting the market?
4 Name three of the main categories of segmentation that a business will use.
5 How do businesses use market segmentation to help create a customer profile for their products? Explain your answer.
6 Write a definition of customer profiling.

Read about it

www.bbc.com/bitesize/guides/zd4kq6f/revision/4 – Tips on market research

www.tutor2u.net/business/reference/market-segmentation – Guidance on market segmentation

LO2 Be able to complete market research to aid decisions relating to a business challenge

For this learning outcome you will learn about the different types of market research and why it is important to complete such research. You also will learn how market research can help a business make important decisions about the products it produces for its existing and new customers.

Teaching content

In this learning outcome you will:

2.1 Carry out market research

2.2 Review the results of market research

2.1 Carry out market research

How to select appropriate research methods

There are two different forms of market research.

Primary research – this is when a business researches information for its own use and for a specific reason. The information required does not yet exist, so will be original for that business. For example:

> A business may devise a questionnaire to ask people particular questions about a specific product.

⬇

> The results of primary research will be up-to-date and unique for that business and should help it to produce a product or service that people will want and which will eventually be profitable.

> An advantage of primary research is that the business can determine precisely the type of information needed and so construct a method of obtaining this information in a form that will suit the people being asked the questions.

> A drawback of primary research is that it can be expensive and time-consuming to complete.

Secondary research – this is research that already exists. It can take many forms, including competitor research, articles in magazines or newspapers and government and industry reports. Today, the internet is the most widely used source of secondary research data. Think about how many times you have been asked to research a topic for school and have used an internet search engine to find out information. You probably found that some of the information you came across was very detailed and not exactly what you were

Getting started

In pairs, think about how you could find out what was the most popular drink sold to young people aged 11 to 16 years in 2018? How would you find out what is the most popular drink purchased by the people in your business class? Share your answers with your class.

looking for. This is the downside of using research that has already been completed. Secondary research can be used to get an overall understanding of a particular market or used as the basis for primary research. When using secondary research, it is important to check how old the data is, as sometimes it can be really out of date and therefore less helpful. The market for a product can change very quickly, so a business will want to ensure its product is still relevant (remember how popular loom bands were a few years ago!) Another reason why secondary research is less useful is that it is likely to have been carried out for a different purpose than that required by the business.

When a business needs to complete some research, it first needs to identify the overall purpose of the research. For example, a crisp manufacturer may want to find out which is the most popular flavour of crisps for people aged 12 to 15 years.

> **Once a business has decided on its research aims, it needs to decide *how* to gather this information. In the case of researching the most popular flavour of crisps, the company might decide to ask people aged 12 to 15 years to answer some questions – perhaps face-to-face or by completing a survey on their mobile phone. The company would then need to think about the best way to reach this target group.**

⇩

> **A business also needs to think about where the research will be completed. If primary research is to be undertaken, then it is important that the researchers visit an area where there are likely to be people in the target group, otherwise the research will be lacking in detail. Returning to the crisps example mentioned above, researchers might select a shopping area on a Saturday afternoon, rather than a Thursday afternoon when the target customers will be in school.**

⇩

> **All researchers will need to be paid, so ensuring that their time is used effectively is also a consideration when completing research as primary research can be costly. Once the results of the research have been analysed, the business will use the information to ensure that its products or services appeal to the customer profile.**

On page 73 we established that businesses use customer profiling to ensure that they produce products that they know will appeal because of the knowledge that they have about their customers. A business will use some of the information from market segmentation to help build a profile of the customers.

Activity

A children's author wants to create a new series of books aimed at 10 to 12 year olds. They have some ideas of themes but are not sure if they will appeal to the target audience. Advise the author about the market research they could complete, giving some practical suggestions.

It is important that a business understands the needs and wants of its customers so all the products appeal to its target market. A typical customer profile will contain information such as:

Age: the age range that a typical customer will be.

Home: where the person may live/type of home.

Occupation: what the customer may do for a living.

Income level: How much they may earn from their job.

Interests: what a typical customer might like to do in their spare time, for example outdoor sports.

Purchases: what the customer likes to purchase and from which businesses.

Once a business has this important information, they can then use this customer profile to target its products at similar customers. This will then ensure that the products produced will be purchased by its like-minded customers.

Using appropriate market research tools (physical or digital) for a business challenge

There are a number of primary and secondary research methods that can be used by an organisation. This section begins by looking at primary research methods. Secondary research methods include competitor research, government publications and published literature.

Surveys/questionnaires
A survey or questionnaire provides a list of questions in order to gain people's views and opinions on a particular subject. A questionnaire is likely to include the following:

- **Closed questions** – the answers to a question are limited, sometimes just to 'yes' and 'no'. Although these questions are quick to answer, they provide little information especially if detailed research is needed, for example: 'Do you eat crisps? Answer: Yes/No'
- **Open questions** – the person answering the question can provide further information in relation to their answer and given their own opinion, for example: 'Describe your ideal crisp. Answer: I like unusual flavours of crisps such as vegetable crisps as they are very crunchy and I like them to be quite spicy.'
- **Multiple choice** – these questions ask the person responding to the questionnaire to select one or multiple answers, depending on the instructions, for example: 'Where do you mostly buy your crisps? Please select one answer from the following: School/Supermarket/Local shop/Petrol station.'
- **Scale or rank questions** – these ask a person to rank their answer to a particular question on a sliding scale, for example: 'Please place the following crisp flavours in order of your favourite (1) to your least favourite (5) – Ready Salted/Cheese and Onion/Salt and Vinegar/Chicken/Chilli.'

Focus group

A focus group involves people being selected to discuss a product or service in a group setting, in order to gain their opinions. A focus group is typically between 6 and 10 people. The topics/subjects of discussion will be planned by the person who wants to find out specific information. There will be a person who guides and facilitates the group of people to enable them to give their own opinions about a particular product or service. Everyone will be encouraged to participate. For example, a business might ask a focus group to examine a new product it wants to launch. The focus group can be used to test out ideas and gather opinions on whether the product is liked or needed by the target audience and whether improvements could be made to it.

Observations

Observations involve customers being watched by researchers while they undertake a specific activity such as shopping. For example, if a supermarket wants to change the layout of some of the aisles to try to increase sales of a specific product, customers could be observed to see if the change results in more of the products being sold. A substantial amount of research by supermarkets has shown that the end of aisles where special offers are often placed are the ones that often have high sales for the duration of the product being placed there. How many times have you seen a good offer and bought it in a supermarket?

Interviews

Interviews involve people being asked a series of questions face-to-face in order to gain their opinions. The interviews may happen in the street, at an agreed location, on the telephone or by other digital means such as Skype or Facetime. The responses will include the opinions of the person who was interviewed. These opinions can then be analysed to determine if the product or service needs to be changed in some way, for example, in relation to price, design or packaging. Interviews enable a business to really get the views of consumers which is an important part of research.

Test marketing

Test marketing is a method of research that a business may use before launching a new product to the whole market. A product could be placed into a limited number of shops to see if consumers show any interest in the product and purchase it. A business could advertise the product within the shop for a limited time and then see how many products are sold within a certain timescale. The results will then be analysed and the business will use these to decide if the test marketing has worked and it is worth rolling out the new product to all stores.

Case study

How M&S is getting 'more bang for its buck' in marketing

Marks & Spencer (M&S) has cut its marketing budget as it looks to get 'more bang for its buck' through an increased focus on social media and its Sparks loyalty card.

The retailer spent £162.7m on marketing in its financial year to 1 April, £23m or 12.6% less than the year before. And while its CFO, Helen Weir, would not be drawn on budgets for this year, she said effectiveness is improving, with M&S getting more for less from its advertising campaigns.

Using loyalty to drive effectiveness

It is not just social media that has helped M&S improve the effectiveness of its marketing. Its Sparks loyalty card has enabled it to speak directly with customers and reduce waste. The scheme now has 5.8 million members, with CEO, Steve Rowe, stating there is plenty of room for more growth given 30 million people actively shop with the brand. And he said Sparks has helped reduce promotional marketing by enabling the retailer to personalise offers. M&S cut two of its big clearance events last year, and has moved away from promotional lines that were not working during events such as Black Friday. 'One of the key points about Sparks is that we want to move away from promotional discounts, big discounts, and use that money much more carefully to give customers the right promotions that extend their loyalty to the business and move them up the value chain,' he told *Marketing Week*. 'Part of that decrease in marketing is due to the reduction in promotional marketing and using Sparks in a much more sensible way.'

Promoting M&S's similarities, not its differences

M&S wants to 'recover and grow' clothing by improving quality, style and authority, while at the same time continuing to grow food. And the retailer claims Sparks is helping it better understand its customers and their shopping habits and therefore to solidify its strategy.

The retailer has carried out more than 700 000 customer interviews either online or in person over the past year, now speaking to a customer 'every 5 seconds'. And it used that insight to inform the launch of its new unified brand message 'Spend it Well', which launched earlier this month. What that research threw up is that there are more similarities than differences across M&S shoppers and its different departments and it needed to start celebrating those, according to Rowe. 'Lots of people talk about the differences [in our brands] but we talk about the similarities. But I think we have probably exaggerated those differences by having two different marketing campaigns,' he explained. 'What we're saying is we're one business, customers see us as one business and so its right to have one unified campaign.'

While the campaign has only been in market for a couple of weeks, Rowe said he is pleased with how it has landed and that it has had the best reaction of any of its campaigns on social media, with 86% of responses positive.

Source: *Marketing Week*

Questions

1 How much had Marks and Spencer's marketing budget been reduced by?

2 What type of marketing campaign did they focus on?

3 What research did they complete prior to launching these new campaigns?

4 Why is it important for a company like Marks and Spencer to complete market research?

Activity

Your school is considering installing two counter snack bars, with lunch time staff serving each customer. The purpose of the snack bars is to ease queuing in the main dining hall which has become a problem lately.

The proposed snack bars will be named the 'Snack Shack' and will stock a variety of chilled products which will be available to purchase as three different choices of 'Snack Pack'. These packs will be prepared in advance and contained in a recyclable paper bag. They will be labelled Pack one, Pack two and Pack three. The cost will be the same for each pack. The school has won local awards for its approach to healthy eating so this does need to be considered. The school also want to consider the packaging of all items within the Snack Pack to create as little waste as possible.

Prepare a questionnaire to determine answers to the following:

1 The items that should go into the Snack Pack.
2 The price the Snack Pack should be sold for (think about the cost of producing it).
3 How often pupils would choose this option at lunchtime.
4 Any other information that you think would be needed to help the school make this idea a success.

Think about who you would ask as you need to make sure that this idea appeals to the whole school community for it to be successful.

A further type of market research is to use secondary research methods. Some examples of secondary research methods include:

- **The internet** – search engines can be used to find out all sorts of data and statistics as well as information on potential competitors. It is important that a business researches who their customers might be and what these competitors are therefore producing. A business cannot copy exactly what a competitior produces, so by completing competitor research, a business will know if their ideas are original and hopefully be able to generate sales from the products they produce. Completing secondary research on the internet means that it can be accessed when it is convinent for the individuals who are involved in the business.

- **Existing market research findings** – it is possible to use the results of research that has already been completed by others in the same market. Such data is often published by businesses such as Mintel (**http://www.mintel.com/**) who specialise in a variety of differnet forms of market research which can be very usfeul for business. Other similar organisations that produce exisiting market research findings are Keynote and Euromonitor.
  - The Office for National Statistics is an independent organisation that collates and publishes a variety of different statistics. The statistics are about the economy, the population and society in the the UK (**https://www.ons.gov.uk**).

Stretch activity

The case study mentions that Marks and Spencer launched its own loyalty card called 'Sparks'. Loyalty cards enable a business like Marks and Spencer to understand what products customers purchase. Consider how this information can be used to help Marks and Spencer. Make notes on the advantages and disadvantages for both Marks and Spencer and its customers of introducing this new loyalty card.

Stretch activity

Write a short report to explain why a questionnaire was appropriate for the Snack Shack idea. Justify your choice of questions and explain what you hope your questionnaire will achieve.

Activity

We are very reliant on the internet these days. This was demonstrated in November 2018 when the O2 network did not work for one day meaning many customers were unable to use their smart phones including accessing the internet. This affected companies who used the network for their business, from taxi drivers to large businesses as well as indivuduals. Research this situation that occurred in November 2018 and report your findings back to your class.

- **Published data** – this can be produced by experts a particular subject that they have extensive knowledge on. They often contain original research. Examples might include the latest research on the progress of reading and writing for 7 to 9 years olds in England's primary schools in a particular part of the country, or medical research on a particular illness and the findings of this research.

- **Newspaper and magazine articles** – these may be useful for a business to discover the opinions of others as well as information on what competitors are doing. Such articles do not have to adhere to strict guidelines so are often an opinion rather than fact. However, they can still be very useful for secondary research especially when starting a new business venture.

- **Government publications** – these are official documents that are produed by the UK government for anyone to access and can be found on the government website (**https://www. gov.uk/government/publications**) and cover a wide range of different areas from consumer product safety to smart meters. Businesses may use these official publications as part of their secondary research. Governments will also consult on issues before writing laws that aim to deal with them. These processes are known as green papers for consultation and white papers for proposals. Any proposed changes to laws will have to be passed through Parliament so will be legally binding.

Using sampling methods

Sampling involves selecting a certain number of people, chosen from a particular group, in order to find out about the whole group. The selected people are asked their opinions on a product or service and the results of this research is assumed to reflect the opinions of the group as a whole. Sampling is useful because it would be impractical and very expensive for a business to find out the opinions of everybody.

There are several ways that a sample can be chosen by a business.

Random sampling
As the name suggests, people are chosen by chance (random). For the purposes of a random survey that was completed in the street, a researcher would stop a number of people as they passed by. The researcher would continue to do this in a particular time frame or until they had obtained information from a required number of participants. The type of participant taking part could not be determined before the research was carried out and so those taking part would represent a cross-section of people's views.

Cluster sampling
This is when the research group is separated into smaller groups known as clusters. For example, a business may choose to separate the country into different geographical areas, such as the South West, the North East, the Midlands, etc. It would then ask research questions in each different cluster. Cluster sampling can be very

Key term

Sampling A method of selecting consumers in order to gain their opinions on a product or service. Types of sampling include random, cluster, quota and convenience

useful as people's opinions and preferences may vary according to where they live. For example, a new product may not appeal to those in the South West cluster compared to the North East cluster because of different tastes.

Quota sampling

This is when the population is separated into a number of different groups who share the same characteristics. This could mean the age and the sex of the group for one segment, while the next segment could be based on outdoor lifestyle interests and hobbies. A researcher might undertake research aimed at one type of quota sample before asking questions of the next agreed quota sample. This can be quite a quick method of sampling for a business, so may be relatively cheap, but it should be used with caution as it does not always represent the views of the whole population.

Convenience sampling

This is a quick and easy way of gathering research in one specific location only, so is convenient for the researcher. Examples of convenience sampling might be carrying out research in your school, workplace, a club that you attend or a shopping centre. (Think back to the questionnaire activity on page 80 about the 'Snack Packs' where your sample was going to be the school community – this is a form of convenience sampling.) Because of the ease of gaining this type of research, the results may not represent the population as a whole, so this needs to be considered.

Activity

In small groups, think of a new product or service that could be offered by each of the following:

- snack bar
- street vendor selling drinks
- cleaning business
- gardening service.

Each business will need to find out some information from consumers about the proposed new product or service and will need to use sampling techniques to do this. Copy and complete the table below. You must use a different type of sampling method for each product or service. Share your business and sampling ideas with the class.

Description of proposed new product/service	Type of sampling method to be used	Explanation of why this sampling method is appropriate for the proposed new product/service

2.2 Review the results of market research

It is all very well completing primary research, but once the results are in, what can you do with this information? A business will analyse the data it has collected and review the research results and use this information to develop the business. There are four processes involved in reviewing the results of any research, as described in Figure 2.3.

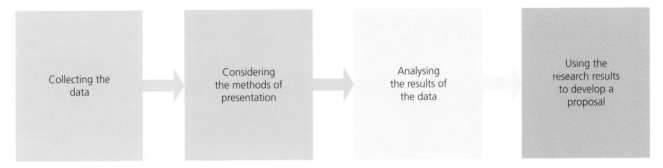

Figure 2.3 Reviewing market research

Stage 1 Collating the data

The first stage of the process is to gather (collate) all the research results together. The responses to questions will be looked at to ensure they are 'clean'. This is because sometimes responses to a survey may not be that honest, answers may not make sense or responders may have rushed the questionnaire and not filled in all the parts correctly. These results would be deemed to be 'unclean' and would therefore be removed.

The remaining data is then collated, usually by inputting the results into a computer to make analysis of the data easier, quicker and more reliable. The results can be presented in many different forms, depending on the needs of those who will be interested in the results. Collating and inputting the data takes time, especially if the sample size is large (for more on sample sizes, see Unit R064, Primary research, page 9). Accuracy is important when collating data.

Stage 2 Methods of presentation

People often have strong preferences for how research findings are presented. Using a computer to input market research data will enable you to select a variety of methods of presentation, including pie charts, graphs and bar charts. Presenting data in a graphical format enables your audience to see results quickly, providing your chosen method is clear and easy to understand.

Activity

1 Look at the following pieces of data that were obtained as a result of market research:

- A survey showed that one in three people said they liked to visit the cinema on a warm summer's day, because it was cooler.
- According to an article in the *Independent* newspaper, in September 2017, industry data showed that 'ketchup sales fell 2.7 per cent to £145.5 million in the UK while volumes fell by 4.2 per cent.'
- Look at the following graph.

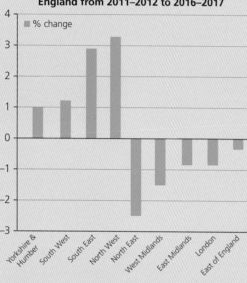

Change in household waste recycling rates in England from 2011–2012 to 2016–2017

2 On a scale of 1 to 3 (where 1 is best and 3 is worst) rate each piece of data in terms of its presentation.

3 Discuss your answers with your neighbour and share the reasons with the class.

Activity

Look at the graph below, then answer the questions.

Estimated value of the world's most valuable brands in 2017 (in billion US$)

Apple	184.15
Google	141.70
Microsoft	80.00
Coca-Cola	69.73
Amazon	64.80
Samsung	56.25
Toyota	50.29
Facebook	48.19
Mercedes-Benz	47.83
IBM	46.83

1 Which is the most valuable brand according to the graph?

2 How much more is Microsoft worth than Amazon according to the graph?

3 What is the second to last least valuable brand according to the graph?

4 How much was Coca-Cola worth in 2017?

Although data presented in graphical format can be very useful, including too many graphs and charts can be confusing to an audience, especially if the information contained within them is irrelevant or is difficult to understand. Always remember to present data in a format that is most suitable for your audience.

Activity

Look at the pictogram below. The research question that was asked was: 'How many people own different types of pet?'

What do you think about the results shown in this pictogram? Is there anything wrong with it?

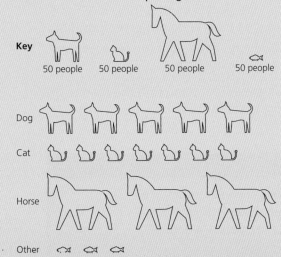

The pictogram shown on the previous page is a little confusing, because if a respondent did not have a pet, how can their response be shown? The pictures are all different sizes, for example, the horse is huge in comparison to the fish and much bigger than the cat. A person might then interpret the results that the horse was the most popular pet. A better example of the pictogram is shown below.

Why is this second pictogram better than the previous one? Discuss your answer with a partner.

Stage 3 Analysing the results of the data

Once you have input your data and decided how to present it, it must be reviewed to work out what it shows. Particular facts and patterns may emerge that are very useful. For example, if most people responded in a survey that they want to purchase your product online rather than in high street stores, then you will know this is the best way to sell your product. Research may also reveal other information, for example:

- 19 out of 20 people responded saying that they preferred product A to product B.
- over half of respondents ranked product D as their most preferred product and product C as their least preferred product.
- over 75 per cent of the people who responded to the survey were disappointed with product E.

The new information obtained as a result of analysing the results of data will help you to develop a proposal for your business – this is the final stage of market research.

Activity

Return to the Snack Packs activity you completed earlier (page 80). The results of some of your questions have now been collated and the findings are displayed below.

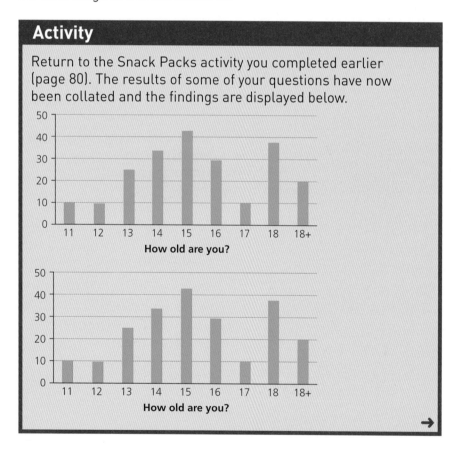

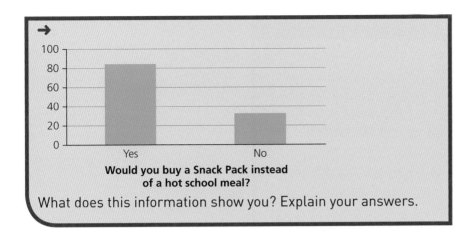

What does this information show you? Explain your answers.

Stage 4 Using the results to develop a proposal

Once all the research findings have been collated, it is important that the data obtained enables you to move to the final stage, which is to develop a proposal. To do this, you need to interpret, analyse and explain your research findings and then develop recommendations for the proposal. The key steps are as follows:

1 Interpret the results of the research.

2 Analyse the results to determine how the data can be used.

3 Consider the original research aims – what questions did you want answers to?

4 How did you try to find answers to these questions?

5 How can the information discovered be presented?

6 What does this information suggest for the future and how can you move forward with it?

7 What is your proposal (may also be called a conclusion) as a result of these research findings?

Activity

Working in groups, develop a proposal using the information from the Snack Packs activities on page 80 and 86. Consider your answers to the following questions:

1 What was the initial problem within the school that made it think about another option?

2 What was the proposed idea?

3 How did you go about trying to find out if this idea might work within the school?

4 How was some of the data analysed?

5 What did some of the main results show?

6 What could you do with this data in order to form a proposal to move forward?

Stretch activity

Write a proposal to the head teacher that covers the main findings of the research. Outline what you propose the school should now do and the timescales involved.

Test your knowledge

1 What is the difference between primary research and secondary research?
2 What is market research?
3 Name three different forms of primary research.
4 Name four different examples of secondary research.
5 Give an example of an open question you can use in a questionnaire.
6 Write a brief explanation of what is meant by sampling.
7 Describe three methods of sampling.
8 Your manager asks you to find out how much the local supermarket is selling a 2 litre bottle of water for. What methods could you use to find out this information?

Read about it

www.tutor2u.net/business/reference/why-is-market-research-needed –
Guidance on the need for market research

https://www.bbc.com/bitesize/guides/zy9frwx/revision/2 –
Guidance on collecting data

www.tutor2u.net/business/reference/marketing-primary-market-research –
explanation of the different methods of primary research

www.bl.uk/business-and-ip-centre/articles/effective-sampling-techniques-for-market-research – Advice from the British Library on sampling techniques

LO3 Be able to develop a design proposal for a business challenge

For this learning outcome you will consider the importance of product designs and how these should be reviewed to meet the requirements of potential customers. You will also learn about different creative techniques and how these can aid business design as well as the importance of gaining feedback. Feedback on an idea is important, as another person may interpret your design in a different way, so a 'fresh pair of eyes' could really help with your design proposal.

Teaching content

In this learning outcome you will:

3.1 Produce product designs for a business challenge

3.2 Review product designs

3.1 Produce product designs for a business challenge

Product design is one of the most important stages of planning a product launch, because without a **design**, how will you know if people will purchase the product? It is important to note that in this unit, you will not be tested on your artistic skills, so professional designs will not gain more marks than a more simplistic design.

Take a look at the following initial designs (also known as **prototypes**) of some well-known products.

DESIGN.

A. SAMUELSON.

BOTTLE OR SIMILAR ARTICLE.
APPLICATION FILED AUG. 18, 1915.

48,160.

Patented Nov. 16, 1915.

FIG. 1.

FIG. 2.

Figure 2.4 Pencil sketch of the Coca-Cola bottle, dating from 1915

Key terms

Design An initial sketch or drawing for a product that can be developed over time

Prototype A physical object produced from a design to determine whether it meets the original concept and can be developed further. Often many prototypes have to be produced before the final idea works

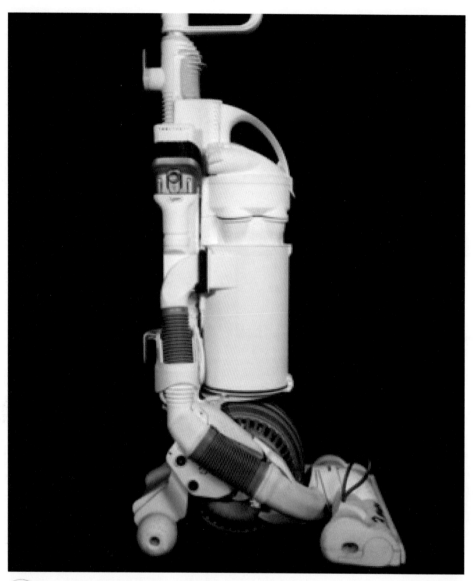

Figure 2.5 Early design for the Dyson vacuum cleaner

 Case study

James Dyson, inventor and designer

Read the following interview with James Dyson, inventor and designer, and Peter Gammack, director of design at Dyson.

'In the late 1970s, I bought the most powerful vacuum cleaner on the market – the Hoover Junior. I got irritated when it started losing suction and tore the bag open. Its pores were clogged with dust: a fundamental flaw, but valuable to the industry because it meant consumers continually had to buy new bags. At the time, consumables were worth something like £500m a year.

Then one day I was at a local sawmill and noticed how the sawdust was being removed from the air by large industrial cyclones. My engineering instinct kicked in. Could that work on a smaller scale? So I created a cardboard prototype and strapped it on to my machine. It didn't look great, but it picked up more dust. Fifteen years and 5 000 prototypes later, I had a bagless vacuum cleaner. By that point, though, I was heavily in debt and didn't know where to turn to bring my machine to the market. Then I received a call from a Japanese company, Apex. I got on a flight and, after several all-night meetings, signed a deal. In 1986, production of what we called G-force began. It looked quite different from the final Dyson design – it was bright pink – but it won a prize and was very successful in Japan. Twenty-two months later, we launched the DC01, the first Dyson vacuum cleaner. It was soon a bestseller.

My wife, Deirdre, and I had moved to the countryside in the 1970s to set about renovating a dilapidated farmhouse. Having to use a wheelbarrow so much, I couldn't get over how bad the design was: the wheel would get stuck or clogged with dirt, and the barrow was made of metal, which went rusty and dented walls. So I added a plastic ball instead of a wheel, which increased stability and manoeuvrability. I called it the Ballbarrow; the design is still a large part of our vacuum machines today.

People have praised the look of Dyson products – our use of bright colours and clear plastic, the industrial appearance – and the vacuum has been called a design icon. I'm flattered that people consider it as such. But I'm a firm believer in function over form. You quickly fall out of love with something that's easy on the eye if it doesn't do the job.'

'We think a lot about design [explains Peter Gammack], but appearance always goes hand in hand with how something works. James wanted a clear bin so you could see how much dust the machine was picking up. Many people were uncomfortable with that idea – who wants to look at the nasty stuff you're sucking off the floor – but he stuck to his guns and it's now a hallmark piece of design. We coloured the handles and the parts you interact with yellow to make it clear that's what they were for. We were proud of the fact that if you pull the handle

out, it turns into a hose – that kind of thing is satisfying, very neat.

I worked on the DC02, the second vacuum, which came a lot more quickly than the first – two years as opposed to 15, with a team of six design engineers working closely with James. The idea was to make a compact model, so you could perch it on stairs. It didn't help that our lab was broken into one day and all our computer-aided design stations stolen. We had to go back to the drawing board, redrawing a lot from scratch. I am a bit surprised that people now think of it as a piece of iconic design, and want to put it in museums and the like. You're just thinking about the product. But it's flattering, of course.

We got sick of big, bulky motors, so we decided to design our own, which needed an investment of something like £250m. We ended up having to develop our own robots because of the precision required. We're set to make one every 4.6 seconds this year. It sounds obvious, but it's so rewarding when all the work culminates in a prototype that actually performs properly. It's not as easy as it looks.

Source: *The Guardian* (24 May 2016)

Questions

1 What was the issue that inspired James Dyson to design a new type of vacuum cleaner?

2 How many prototypes did James Dyson create before going into production?

3 How many years did it take James Dyson to produce the product?

4 Why has the product been praised and identified as a 'design icon'?

5 How long did it take to produce the DC02 vacuum?

6 What issues did the business face when designing the DC02 model?

Why draft product designs are produced

Draft designs are a crucial stage of the product design process, because seeing a sketch or a picture of a design can bring it to life. A sketch can then be used to produce a prototype, which is the first version of a physical product using the design. As highlighted in the case study, James Dyson made 5000 prototypes before producing his final product. This shows why the product design stage is so important – it is unlikely a design will be completely right first time and many prototypes will need to be made before the final product is ready.

Stretch activity

What are the main lessons you have learnt from reading the James Dyson case study? Explain your answer.

Figure 2.6 shows the methods used by businesses to gain important knowledge from the design stage of producing a product.

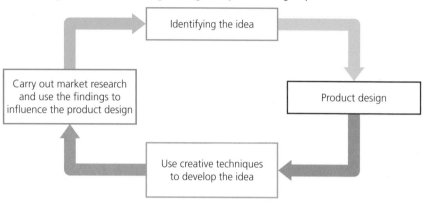

Figure 2.6 The design stage of producing a product

All the areas shown in Figure 2.6 are important for different reasons.

- The first stage of identifying the idea comes from a business finding a gap in the market for a particular product. If you look at the market as a whole, there are many different products to choose from – for example, think about the many different kinds of toothpaste that are available to buy.

- Product design enables the business to put the idea into some form of sketch, which as a result of further research, can then be adapted.

- Creative techniques are then used to develop the idea and turn the sketch into a design which might form the basis for a prototype. A prototype is when a sketch or design is turned into a physical object for people to see and touch. This makes a sketch come to life and is a very exciting phase, especially if you came up with the idea.

- Carrying out market research might involve questioning people who would be interested in purchasing the product in the future. The results of this market research will be used to help improve the design of the proposed product.

Activity

Look at the image.

1 In pairs, discuss what famous branded product you think this is the equivalent of today.

2 If you presented this as a prototype, what five questions would you ask your potential customers so that your idea could be improved? Share your ideas with your class.

How to produce designs for a business challenge to meet the market need

Relating designs to market research findings

Having a vision for a new design of a product is a great start but what happens if it does not appeal to potential customers? This is when market research is really useful and it needs to be completed before the design is finalised. In the Dyson Case study on page 90, it was clear that the original design was developed over many years. This is because customer needs and wants changed during this period. Dyson customers now have a choice of different products but the overall technology used has remained the same. Extensive market research was completed by Dyson which helped when developing the newer products.

Relating designs to the business challenge brief

When a business is designing a new product, it is important that they complete some form of market research based around the original product brief because if the design does not appeal to customers, it will not sell.

In the 1980s, Kellogg's wanted to launch a new breakfast cereal – this was their business challenge. However, they recognised that the breakfast cereal market is very competitive. When Kellogg's introduced Crunchy Nut Cornflakes, they knew that they had to get the design of the product right for customers to purchase the cereal. Kellogg's used a form of taste testing for their market research where consumers were asked a series of questions about the product as they tasted the cereal. The product design was then developed according to the results of the market research. Kellogg's understood that the overall design in terms of the packaging, look and taste of the product had to be right in order for the new product to sell. Kellogg's research paid off, because in 2017, Crunchy Nut Cornflakes was the second most popular Kellogg's cereal consumed in the UK.

It is important that the market research completed by any business is meaningful. This means that the business can go back to their original designs to update them as a result of the market research to ensure that they meet the design brief. If this is not completed, the business may design a product that does not appeal to their target market.

Identifying and using creative techniques

Creative techniques can be used to help develop your business ideas, as outlined below.

● **Mind maps** – these provide a visual summary of your ideas for the product (see Figure 2.7). The product idea appears in the centre of the diagram, and then other aspects of the product (known as sub-topics) are drawn around the central product idea. These are circled and linked back to the product idea with lines or arrows. Examples of sub-topics could include the features of the product, the target audience, how much to charge, where to purchase the product, design ideas, etc. Then, using the sub-topics, complete

Figure 2.7 Making a mind map

93

the process again, adding more circles and arrows to show the development of your thinking. With a mind map, you can use different colours, change the size of the writing and have different lengths of lines – the more visual the better, and you can really make it your own.

Activity

Think about your morning routine on a school day and the sequence of events that occurs. Draw a mind map of your routine with the main circle in the middle labelled 'Getting to school'. Include sub-topics and link them with lines to make a mind map. Share your mind map with the rest of the class.

Stretch activity

Look at five different mind maps produced by others in your class.

1 What do you notice that is different about them?

2 What do you think works well? What doesn't work so well?

3 Note down your findings and produce a short guide on how to complete a mind map.

- **Mood boards** – these are used by a designer to record all their visual ideas in one place (see Figure 2.8). They contain a variety of images, sketches and other ideas. A mood board will often include different types of materials and colours – each board is unique. They enable the designer to review all their different ideas and then select the key ones for their product design.

  To create a mood board, you need to consider the following:

  ○ What will you use for the basis of your mood board – paper, cardboard, wood? You might decide to create a digital mood board.

  ○ How will you separate your ideas? You could add borders or maybe you would prefer a collage effect?

  ○ Will colour be one of the key parts of your mood board?

  ○ What size text will you use?

  ○ Will you include samples of materials on your mood board? If so, where will you get these from?

Figure 2.8 Mood board

- **SCAMPER model** – this is a tool that enables you to think about creating new products/services from ones that already exist. The acronym SCAMPER stands for:

  ○ **S**ubstitute – could you use this product as an alternative for something else? What materials or items could you substitute to improve your product design? Is there anything extra that you might want to add in?

  ○ **C**ombine – if you were to combine this product with something else, it could become something new. To maximize the uses of a product, what could you combine it with?

  ○ **A**dapt – what could you do to adapt the product so it can be used for another reason or purpose? Is this product similar to another? What other products could you look at to gain inspiration?

  ○ **M**odify – what could you do to specifically change the shape, look or feel of this product? What could you do to the product to add value to it? Could you use materials that would be more environmentally friendly? Could it be recycled?

○ **P**ut to another use – could you use this product somewhere else? Could others use the product in a different situation? Could the waste produced by making the product be recycled or made into something else?

○ **E**liminate – thinking about the existing product, is there any way that you could simplify it to make it easier to use? Could you make it work faster, be smaller/lighter/brighter? If you took away one feature of the product, would it change it much? Would it make it even better? Could you have something different instead?

○ **R**everse – if you did the opposite of what you think might work at the moment, what impact would this have on the product? Could you do the process in reverse order or reorganise the sequence of the process?

Figure 2.9 Camping chairs were originally designed for people who went camping, but these days they are used at outdoor events, picnics and on the beach. The original concept of a chair specifically for camping has changed into an outdoor chair for anyone to use.

Activity

Consider the first generation iPad created by Apple in 2010. Using the SCAMPER tool, how has Apple designed the latest version of the iPad to create something new that people want to purchase?

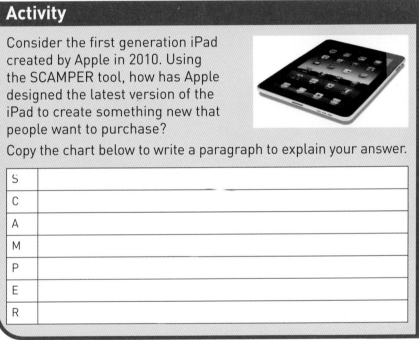

Copy the chart below to write a paragraph to explain your answer.

S	
C	
A	
M	
P	
E	
R	

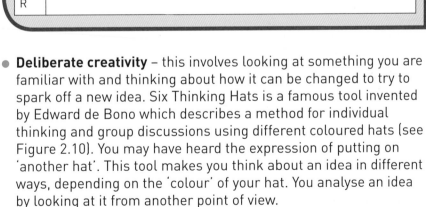

● **Deliberate creativity** – this involves looking at something you are familiar with and thinking about how it can be changed to try to spark off a new idea. Six Thinking Hats is a famous tool invented by Edward de Bono which describes a method for individual thinking and group discussions using different coloured hats (see Figure 2.10). You may have heard the expression of putting on 'another hat'. This tool makes you think about an idea in different ways, depending on the 'colour' of your hat. You analyse an idea by looking at it from another point of view.

○ White hat – if you are wearing this hat, look at the data you have – this might include sales information, costs and past trends, etc. The data will help you understand the market.

○ Red hat – if wearing this hat, you will look at the problems associated with the idea, as well as how people do or do not respond to them. You also have to focus on the emotions of others, so you can anticipate their responses. You will need to use your gut instinct – entrepreneurs are known to rely on this.

○ Black hat – this hat makes you think about the issues that could cause a problem and the things that might go wrong with the idea. Although it might seem a negative role, it is important, as many ideas never succeed.

○ Yellow hat – like the effect of the sunshine on most people, this hat is about looking at the best aspects of the design idea. The opposite of the black hat, so has the power of positive thinking.

○ Green hat – if you are wearing this hat then your focus is where this product idea might lead, so you need to think creatively and use lateral thinking. You need to look at an issue and try to create a solution to the problem.

○ Blue hat – this final hat brings all the other coloured hat ideas to the table and manages them. Although you might delegate tasks out to the different hats, you will oversee the process and will maintain control.

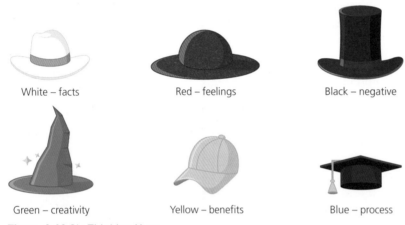

| White – facts | Red – feelings | Black – negative |
| Green – creativity | Yellow – benefits | Blue – process |

Figure 2.10 Six Thinking Hats

Activity

Working in groups of six, allocate one of the coloured 'hats' outlined above to each person so that everyone has a role. Each person should make sure they understand what their role is before discussing the following situation:

The managing director of Jasper Ollie Ltd is considering launching a new product which offers a scooter and children's car seat combined to produce a new type of pushchair with built-in scooter. This idea appeals to the managing director and she has called a meeting to discuss the idea with your team. In preparation, each team member should write down some ideas related to

the type of 'hat' they have been allocated. During the discussion, each member must act according to their hat colour. For example, the black hat is negative so the person with this hat would give negative responses to any comments, such as 'That would be too expensive' and 'Who would buy it?'

Case study

Gandy's

In 2001, Paul and Rob Forkan, aged 11 and 13, and their younger siblings, were taken out of school by their parents to work on humanitarian projects in India. They were on holiday in Sri Lanka on Boxing Day in 2004 when a tsunami wave hit their hotel. The children lost both their parents and were left with nothing.

After returning home to the UK they started to rebuild their lives, supported by family and friends. The brothers completed their education and went travelling, volunteering with local charities in India along the way. However, they were keen to create something unique in honour of their parents who had taught them they should do more in life than just exist. When one of the brothers woke up one night after being at a music festival, he said that his 'mouth felt like one of Gandhi's flip flops'. The brand was born, as Paul and Rob decided to focus on flip flops. They had no idea how to set up a business but their determination, ambition and drive paved the way. Looking at the design of a simple flip flop, they decided to make them more appealing and designed some which were coloured and featured maps as part of the design. They were certainly different to those of competitors. The brothers tried selling online and on beaches, but with little success. Then they approached an independent shop who placed an

order and soon they had 40 outlets selling their flip flops. Gandy's decided to go mainstream and sell via high street stores such as John Lewis.

Today, Gandy's is a successful company with a famous brand, selling flip flops, clothing and accessories. In recognition of the brothers' own experiences, ten per cent of the profits from every pair of flip flops goes to help orphans and underprivileged children affected by the tsunami.

Questions

1 What are the main messages in this case study about the company, Gandy's?

2 Flip flops have been around for many years and yet Gandy's have made a successful brand out of a personal situation that was life-changing for the brothers. Research the company and create an information poster that details their story as well as a variety of different products that they produce and sell. The following websites may help you:

- www.gandyslondon.com/our-journey
- www.independent.co.uk/life-style/fashion/features/gandys-flip-flops-how-the-funky-footwear-brand-was-created-9858349.html
- www.brandalley.co.uk/blog/story-behind-brand-gandys- flip-flops/

3.2 Review product designs

When a designer produces a product, it is highly unlikely that their first attempts at design will meet all the requirements of their potential customers. Reviewing the product design is therefore an essential part of the development of a new product. Designs can therefore be reviewed in several different ways.

How to review designs for a business challenge

Gaining feedback

Feedback is an important aspect of learning. Think about when you complete a piece of homework, play in a football match, audition for a part in a play or compete in a competition. In each case, someone will review your performance and provide both positive and negative comments as part of the review, which could be from an adult such as your teacher or coach, or fellow team members or members of your class. Balanced feedback – both positive and negative – enables us to keep learning throughout our lives. You may consider using two or three different forms of feedback, such as self-assessment, feedback from others and peer assessment (asking friends and other students to assess and provide feedback).

Self-assessment

This involves looking at your designs and critically assessing your product. A simple form of self-assessment that is quick and easy to complete is a SWOT analysis. A SWOT analysis requires you to look at a product's **s**trengths, **w**eaknesses, **o**pportunities and **t**hreats and group these under the headings shown in Figure 2.11.

Strengths	**Weaknesses**
• Environmentally-friendly materials used • Modern appearance	• Components used are expensive to manufacture, which increases costs • Similar products available on the market
Opportunities	**Threats**
• No other similar products offered by competitors • New markets opening up for this type of product	• Government may introduce legislation which will require product to be made of 75 per cent environmentally-friendly materials

Figure 2.11 SWOT chart showing examples of each category

Strengths and weaknesses of design proposals relating to customer profile

Using the results of a SWOT analysis, especially the strengths and weaknesses, will enable you to review your original design and the customer profile you have identified. Your product must be appealing to the identified audience so that it sells. A product that fails to sell is a waste of the time and money invested in it. Referring back to your original idea and focusing on your customer profile will help you re-focus your design back to the most important people, your potential customers.

The importance of finalising a design after feedback

Once you have gathered some feedback, what should you do with it? This information will be very helpful for you when finalising your design. If the feedback showed that the colour would not appeal to the target market, then that would be an obvious change. Maybe the price you suggested was too expensive, so could you realistically make it cheaper? This may not be possible if you are using more expensive materials, but could you use alternatives more cheaply? Packaging the product will also be an important consideration for the product's overall design and this will need to relate back to your customer profile. For example, if you decide to use environmentally-friendly materials for both the product and packaging, your target market may be willing to pay more, knowing that this product is not damaging the environment.

Modifications may need to be made to your designs as a result of feedback, but it is important to get the product right, so that it appeals to your customer profile and target market.

Activity

Look at the products below and give feedback on the ideas.

Solar-powered seat with USB charger

Table tennis door

Cup clip for tables

Glass holder for a plate

1 Complete a SWOT analysis for each product.
2 Which one of the four products do you think would be the most popular? Why?

Test your knowledge

1 What is a draft design? Explain your answer.
2 Why do you think it is important to produce product designs?
3 What are the main differences between a mind map and a mood board?
4 What does the acronym SCAMPER stand for?
5 What are the Six Thinking Hat colours and what does each one mean?
6 What does the acronym SWOT stand for?
7 How can SWOT analysis help with design?
8 Why is feedback an important aspect of design?

Read about it

www.brainstorming.co.uk/tutorials/scampertutorial.html – Tutorial on how to use SCAMPER

www.mindtools.com/pages/article/newISS_01.htm – Advice on how to use mind maps

www.canva.com/learn/make-a-mood-board/ – Tips for creating a mood board

www.tutor2u.net/business/reference/swot-analysis – Explanation of SWOT analysis

L04 Be able to review whether a business proposal is viable

For this learning outcome, you will learn the importance of identifying and calculating the costs involved in a business proposal. Understanding these costs will help you devise an appropriate selling price for your product and enable you to demonstrate an understanding of break-even and put it into practice. You will also learn about the different pricing strategies that could be used and the risks involved when producing any new product. This will help you determine if the business proposal is realistic and viable.

Teaching content

In this learning outcome you will:

4.1 Calculate the costs involved in a business challenge

4.2 Apply an appropriate pricing strategy

4.3 Review the likely success of a business challenge

4.4 Identify the challenges when launching a new product

Getting started

You have decided to make some individual, handmade wooden boxes to sell at a school enterprise event. The boxes will be designed to go in the garden so that plants can be put in them. You are not sure how much to price the boxes, so need to work out how much each box will cost to make.

In pairs, complete the following tasks:

1 Write a list of all the items (materials) and tools you will need to make a box.

2 The wood you need for each box will cost £1.00. All the other items you have listed, including tools, will cost £2.50. Work out how much each box will cost to make.

3 It is important that you see how much your competitors are selling similar products for. Your box will be 30 cm x 45 cm. Research the costs of similar items, writing the names of the businesses and the cost of the item.

4 Working individually, look at your research and think about your target market. How much do you think you will sell your product for at the school enterprise event?

5 Work out how much profit you will make per box.

6 Working individually, justify why you think this selling price and profit margin is appropriate.

Stretch activity

Thinking about the profit you will make on each wooden garden box. What could you do with this money in terms of future business enterprise opportunities? Write a blog suggesting your thoughts.

4.1 Calculate the costs involved in a business challenge

Cost per unit to make

The 'Getting started' task gave you the opportunity to think about the items that are needed to make a product such as a wooden box. Any item that you purchase will have cost a business an amount of money to make. These costs include raw materials, packaging, delivery, staff wages/salaries, overhead costs (heating, lighting, electricity) and advertising. There is a lot to think about! This is why a business must make sure it can accurately work out the actual cost per product, which is also known as the cost per unit to make. This helps a business to determine the final selling price of a product. Consider the following example:

Jenny makes decorations out of driftwood collected from the beach. Her speciality is making a driftwood tree, which she thinks would be popular at Christmas. She has lots of driftwood, which she collected in the summer months. She also needs a metal pole costing £1.99 and strong glue costing 30p to make each tree. However, each tree takes 1.5 hours to make and Jenny pays herself £9.80 per hour.

1   How much does it cost to make each tree?

2   How many trees could Jenny make in six hours?

3   If Jenny sold her trees for £30 each, how much profit would she make per tree?

Let's work it out:

Jenny's material costs are £1.99 for the pole + 30p for the strong glue = £2.29

Jenny pays herself £9.80 per hour and it takes her 1.5 hours to make a tree. Her labour costs are:

£9.80 + £4.90 (£9.80 ÷ 2 = £4.90) **=** £14.70 for 1.5 hours work.

Jenny's total costs to make one tree are: £2.29 + £14.70 = £16.99

In 6 hours Jenny could make 4 trees as they take her 1.5 hours to make (6 hours ÷ 1.5 hours = 4 trees)

£30.00 (selling price) – £16.99 (total costs) = £13.01 per unit

Activity

For each of the business products below, work out the costs per unit.

1 Business 1: Olivia owns 10 hens. Each day she collects the eggs (usually 9 eggs each day), which her family enjoy. Olivia has decided to start selling the eggs to make some extra pocket money. She knows that the cost of keeping the hens (food, bedding and the coop to keep them safe at night) is £30 per month. Egg boxes cost £5.70 for 50 boxes. Olivia will put 6 eggs in a box to sell.

   a Calculate the cost to Olivia of producing 6 eggs in a box ready to sell to her customers.

2 Business 2: Jamal wants to sell home-made lemonade at the school Summer Fete. He will sell it in recyclable 'drinking cones' as he is concerned about the environment. His mum has a suitable container from which he can dispense the lemonade and she has said he can use it for free. To make 1 litre of lemonade, Jamal will need 4 lemons costing 12p each, 500g sugar which costs 47p, citric acid which costs 45p and water. He has decided to purchase water, which will cost 17p per litre.

   a What is the cost per unit of 1 litre of lemonade?

   b Jamal will make 25 litres in advance – how much will this cost?

   c Jamal has worked out that he can sell 10 cones of lemonade per litre. How much will each cone of lemonade cost?

Proposed selling price per unit

All businesses need to know how much it costs to produce the items they sell. If they do not, they could end up in debt, which would not be good for the business. Selling price is different to the cost per unit – it is how much you are going to sell the product to your customers for.

It is essential to undertake research into competitor pricing before deciding the price at which to sell your own product. This research may include the following.

- Assessing the competition – research how much competitors are selling similar products for. Look for any special deals that competitors are using to sell their products, such as buy one get one free. You could monitor their deals and see if they offer prices at a particular time of year, or if offers are on every month. Consider whether this approach is something you can do to, so you can compete with them.

- Complete research to try and find out which products offer the best value to customers – you could ask customers questions to find out why they buy a particular product compared to another. They may tell you how they decide to purchase a particular item, for example, if low price is the most important factor, or reliability. You could ask if a customer would purchase a product that costs more if it was to last longer? This could help you to see which products are the most successful within certain segments of the market.

- Compare your product to those of competitors – you need to identify what is different about your product compared to others. What are its unique features? What are its benefits? Is it handmade, organic, environmentally friendly, fair trade? People will generally pay more money for such items, providing they are what they say they are.

- Look at the prices of competitor's products and use this as a basis for your product – if your product is very expensive and has exactly the same features as a competitor's product, then why would someone buy your product? If your product is sold at a very cheap price, some customers may not want to purchase your item, as they may think it is not good quality. A product priced too cheaply will mean the business is losing potential profits that could have been made if the product had been priced slightly higher.

- Consider if you could realistically sell the product at a higher price. Is your product better quality, more reliable, better taste (if a food or drink item) or does it have more features? If so, then you could justify charging a higher price. You will need to make sure that you highlight these points so that the product will sell.

- Could you offer a discount to begin with and keep selling the product for a long time? If you decide to offer a discount it is important that customers are aware of this. In supermarkets you often see items on offer but they will say 'limited offer' or 'special discounts' and state when the offer ends. This is so a business can maximise the amount of products they sell during this time period, and then hopefully customers will keep buying the product because they like it or they trust the brand.

Activity

Revisit Business 1 from the Activity on page 102, and the example of Olivia who wants to sell eggs from her hens in boxes of six.

1 Research how much eggs are sold for in a variety of different outlets, e.g. supermarkets, local shops and farm shops. Copy and complete the table below to record your research findings.

Name of business	Cost for six eggs

2 Using this information, as well as the figures you calculated to determine Olivia's unit costs, how much would you advise Olivia to sell her boxes of six eggs for?

Activity

Look at the following products and pricing information.

Vintage electric fan – £46.99   Fun fan – £15.99

Electric standing fan – £24.99   Small fan – £8.99

Using the information from pages 102–103, answer the following questions:

1 Which fan would you purchase?

2 Why would you purchase this fan in comparison with the other three fans? Explain your answer.

3 Who do you think is the target market for each fan? Explain your reasons.

4 Write a description of each fan to try and persuade a potential customer to purchase the fan. Remember to include the price.

Stretch activity

Create an advertising poster that highlight the main features of your chosen fan.

Profit per unit

Profit is the amount of money that a business makes after all the costs have been paid for. For example, if it costs a business 25p to make a product and they sell it for £1.00, the profit per unit is 75p. As a percentage this would be a 75 per cent profit margin per product, which is excellent.

Sometimes a business will state that they make a certain percentage of profit per product or unit, so they know how much money they are making. The business will need to decide what it will do with this profit. It could, for example, re-invest the money into new machinery, develop new products or pay out some of its profits to its shareholders (if it is a public or private limited company).

Knowing the profit per unit can be an incentive to business owners and employees, especially if they know they are making 75 per cent profit on every unit. An understanding of profit per unit can make you see that putting in the extra effort now will really pay off later.

Total costs

Total costs are found when the fixed and variable costs are added together:

Total costs = Fixed cost + Variable costs

A business has to consider a variety of different costs when producing a product to be sold. As well as the costs of the materials to make the products, a business also has to factor in fixed and variable costs.

- **Fixed costs** are costs that do not change, whether you make one unit or one hundred units. Examples of fixed costs are rent for a building, water and power (electricity and gas), council rates, machinery, tools, insurance and specialist equipment. Fixed costs do not increase or when the output from a business changes.
- **Variable costs** change according to a business's level of output. For example, if 50 items are made and then another 20 are needed, the business will need to order in more materials to make the products, which would increase their output. The raw materials and manpower that are used to make the extra output are examples of variable costs.

It is important for a business to know what its total costs are, as this helps determine its eventual selling price.

(For more on fixed costs, variable costs and total costs, see Unit RO64, pages 18–20.)

Total profit

A business will want to calculate the total profit from the sale of its products. In order to do this, it needs to calculate its total revenue and subtract this from the total costs. The calculation for total revenue is:

Total revenue = Output × Price

For example, Sarah sells ice lollies in the summer at an outdoor swimming pool. On a busy day she can sell up to 300 ice lollies. Each ice lolly is sold for £1.50. Sarah's total revenue on a busy day when she sells out of lollies is 300 × £1.50 = £450.

Activity

Look back at the activities that describe businesses involving selling eggs and lemonade (page 102) and making Christmas trees from driftwood (page 101). For each business, identify five variable costs.

Total profit is the amount of money that a business will receive from selling the number of products it has made that are then sold to the customers. The calculation for total profit is:

Total profit = Total revenue – Total costs

Sarah has to pay £20 in rent each day that she sells her ice lollies at the outdoor swimming pool. The rent covers the electricity needed to keep the ice lollies frozen. This cost does not change, so on days when there are not that many people swimming Sarah may not make many sales. However, she still has to pay the £20 rent.

To work out Sarah's total profit on a day when she sells all her ice lollies, you need to complete the sum of:

£450 (total revenue) – £20 (total costs).

Therefore, Sarah's total profit is £430.

Sarah knows that on a busy day she could potentially earn £430. Imagine, however, that it rains most days in the school summer holidays. For Sarah, this would be a disaster, as she would still have to pay the rent to the swimming pool and have ice lollies available to sell to customers, even though she may not make many sales.

Activity

Sarah has decided to increase the prices of her ice lollies. They will now cost £2.00 each and come in a variety of different flavours. The swimming pool have decided to charge her a weekly rent of £150. They also are going to charge her a daily electricity charge, as there have been recent increases to this cost. The charge will be £3.00 per day. Sarah will be at the swimming pool six days a week. Her brother, Thomas, will work on Sarah's day off. He will be paid £45 for the day. Sarah can now store 400 ice lollies in her freezer, which is the maximum she can sell in one day.

Using all the above figures, answer the following questions:

1 Identify which items are fixed costs.
2 How much does Sarah have to pay each week (7 days) for the charges incurred by the swimming pool?
3 Identify Sarah's total costs.
4 If Sarah were to sell the following amount of ice lollies in one week, what would be the total profit she would make? Remember to calculate all her costs.

Day	1	2	3	4	5	6	7
Ice lollies sold	200	400	350	150	225	175	50

4.2 Apply an appropriate pricing strategy

It is important that a business's product sells, otherwise it is a waste of money. Having a warehouse of unsold products costs money, so a business must sell a product that customers want and which is priced correctly. Businesses use a variety of different methods to try and get us to buy their products.

Supermarkets are famous for having different offers on products each week. Both Aldi and Lidl have weeks when they promote products that are on special offer, such as camping and barbeque goods in the summer. These pricing deals are known as **pricing strategies**, because the businesses are trying out different methods to try and get us to part with our money. If one method does not work, then they might try a different one.

Key term

Pricing strategies Different methods of pricing used by businesses to encourage customers to purchase their products

Activity

Think of six different offers you have seen on products on sale in stores recently. What were the products and prices? Were they good deals? Share your answers with the rest of the class.

Case study

Just how 'special' are supermarket special offers?

We're all familiar with the brightly coloured signs displayed in supermarkets – 'limited offer', 'buy one get one free', 'half-price offer'. They encourage us to buy more items, sometimes for things we don't really need, but are these offers as good as they seem?

Supermarkets tell us that we can save money by purchasing multi-buys, but research suggests that sometimes these offers are misleading, because the supermarkets increase the price of a single item just before the offer begins. This results in shoppers spending more per item than they would have done before the offer began. For example, a supermarket might be selling apples at £2 for a pack of six. They could increase the price of the pack of apples to £3.50 and then launch a special offer of two packs for £5. Although the offer price is cheaper than the new price of the apples, shoppers would be spending more for the two items than they would have before the offer began.

Special deals encourage us to buy products even when the saving is quite small or the product is more expensive than our usual brand. Sometimes supermarkets label something as a 'special offer' when in fact it is always sold at or around that price. Buying a discounted product is fine if it is the brand you normally choose, but many people feel the need to 'grab a bargain' when they see it, even if it is for a product they wouldn't usually buy.

So, next time you visit the supermarket and are tempted by a deal, think twice, do the maths and be sure it really is as good as it seems.

Questions

1 What is the main message from reading this case study?

2 Why is important to 'do the maths' before purchasing a special offer product?

3 Design your own supermarket 'not so' special offer sign to try and get people to purchase your favourite product to eat or drink.

Types of different pricing strategies

There are a number of pricing strategies you may consider for your product proposal, as explained below.

Competitive pricing

Competitive pricing involves looking at how much your direct competitors are charging for a particular product and then reducing the price of your product so that customers will purchase your product rather than those of your competitors. This can mean the profit margins you receive are reduced during the time of the special offer, but you should sell lots of products. If a business wants to get rid of old stock to make room for new stock, competitive pricing could be used to sell the old stock that is taking up space in the warehouse. A business will always take into account the price charged by rival organisations, particularly in competitive markets. Setting a price above that charged by the market leader will only work if your product has better features and appearance.

Psychological pricing

How many times have you seen a product that is priced at £9.99? Many people feel they are getting a better deal if they pay £9.99 for a product instead of £10.00, even though there is only 1p difference! This is why so many businesses price their products with 99p at the end instead of a rounded figure. Psychological pricing makes the customer think the product is cheaper than it really is, which helps make a sale.

Price skimming

Price skimming is a method businesses use when introducing a new product that is often unique to the market, so it does not face competition. A high price will be set to maximize profits before other competitors produce similar products and start to move into the market. Price skimming only works for a limited time before competitors launch something similar. Businesses who adopt this approach to selling must ensure they can supply customers with the product so they are not disappointed. Trying to predict the demand for a product is very hard. There have been examples over the years of the demand for products not being met by the businesses, resulting in bad press. However, customers who enjoy being the first to own new products are often willing to pay a high price for what they consider to be the best or latest version of a product.

Price penetration

This is where a business produces a product and initially sets its price very low to attract customers to buy it, with the intention of then increasing the price after the special offer period. Businesses use this method to increase sales when they introduce a new product to the market. The sales may increase if the pricing strategy is successful, but this will affect the profits made within the special offer period, as these are based on a low selling price.

However, if customers like the product, they will then keep purchasing it so the business receives repeat custom. It will also increase the business's share of the market, known as 'market share'. If this happens, then the pricing strategy has worked.

Many brands have a variety of different products that have been developed over the years, which together form a product portfolio. For example, Cadbury has many different chocolate bars in its portfolio, aimed at different areas of the market. If Cadbury wanted to persuade customers to purchase a new product, it might offer a new chocolate bar at a low price during a 'special offer' period. People know and trust the Cadbury brand, and might be willing to try the new chocolate bar. Cadbury would hope that customers would like the chocolate bar and, once sales were established, could raise the price and continue to receive repeat custom. Price penetration is the opposite of price skimming.

 Case study

iPhone X

When Apple launched the iPhone X in 2017, it sold out in less than 10 minutes as a result of pre-orders. The phone initially cost £999 for the basic model, with the most expensive version coming in at £1 149 – more than some models in Apple's MacBook and iMac computer range. Despite this, demand for the new iPhone X was so high that it caused the company's servers to crash as customers tried to purchase the new phone.

Questions

1 What type of pricing strategy have Apple used in this case study? Explain your answer.

2 Research three different business websites to determine how much it now costs for the iPhone X. What pricing strategies are being used by the different businesses?

3 Why do you think these pricing strategies were chosen by the businesses? Do the results surprise you? Explain your answer.

Loss leaders

Loss leaders are when a business sells a product at a price that is less than what it costs to produce. A business will do this to attract customers to visit a particular shop or website in the hope that they will then purchase other products that will enable the business to make a profit. The idea with this strategy is to capitalise on getting the customer through the door or to visit the website. However, there is a possible risk that customers attracted by the loss leader offer will only purchase this one item as it is such a good deal. Buying lots of one product is called bulk buying. To avoid heavy losses, a business may state that customers are limited to purchasing a certain number of the product, for example, five packs per customer only. This tactic helps the business to limit bulk buying by customers and hopefully encourage them to make other purchases. Loss leader is a pricing strategy that is time limited due to the profit margins that will be lost.

(For more on pricing strategy, see Unit RO64, pages 38–39.)

Activity

Look at the products below.

- Yogurt
- Washing-up liquid
- Games console
- Crisps
- Water
- Fizzy drink
- Washing powder
- Chocolate bar
- Chewing gum
- Headphones

1 Research the prices of different brands of each of these products.

2 Copy and complete the table below to record your findings. An example has been completed for you.

Product	Brand name	Name of business	Promotional price	Pricing strategy
Water	Evian	Bargain brands	25p	Loss leader

3 Look for special offers and write a short article for a consumer website that explains the deals of the week that you can find for each of the different forms of pricing strategy. Make sure you include examples of competitive pricing, psychological pricing, price skimming and price penetration.

4.3 Review the likely success of a business challenge

When a new product is to be brought onto the market, a business can save lots of time and effort if it completes proper market research first. This research will enable the business to make important decisions regarding pricing, sales, revenue and profit.

Pricing decision – the eventual pricing decision for the product should be successful if essential market research is completed, because the business will know wheter the target market will like the product and how much they would be willing to pay for it.

Predicted number of sales – market research will enable the business to predict the number of sales from customers when the product is launched. It is important that the business asks questions related to how frequently a potential customer may purchase the product. If the product was a bar of soap for example, a customer may state that they would purchase it more frequently than, say, a football, as soap is a product used daily. Having an idea of the predicted number of sales will enable the business to produce appropriate amounts of stock so that there is enough to meet demand. The technology company Apple have struggled to keep up with demand from customers in the past but in 2018 it was revealed that their sales figures had declined. This shows that sometimes predicted sales are not always correct.

Predicted sales revenue – once predicted sales have been calculated, this can enable a business to then predict the potential sales revenue. They will use the numbers from their predicted sales to help calculate the sales revenue that will be generated from the sales. This will help a business plan their finances.

Predicted profit – predicting the amount of profit generated from selling products is an important aspect of planning a business venture. The predicted sales and sales revenue calculations will need to be used to help identify the predicted profit (total revenue – total costs). A business will then be able to estimate what their finances will look like at the end of a set period of time.

Use break-even analysis in a business challenge

Details of what the break-even point is and the different ways in which it can be calculated is covered in Unit R064 (page 21–24). The example below provides a reminder of how to calculate the break-even point.

Bailey Brown makes small garden tables. His fixed costs are £20 000 and the variable costs are £10 per unit. The selling price for each unit is £60. Bailey's aim is to break even as quickly as possible.

Figure 2.12 shows how Bailey can work out his break-even point.

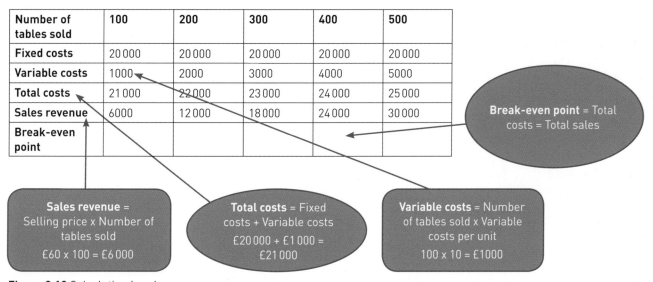

Number of tables sold	100	200	300	400	500
Fixed costs	20 000	20 000	20 000	20 000	20 000
Variable costs	1000	2000	3000	4000	5000
Total costs	21 000	22 000	23 000	24 000	25 000
Sales revenue	6000	12 000	18 000	24 000	30 000
Break-even point					

Break-even point = Total costs = Total sales

Sales revenue = Selling price x Number of tables sold
£60 x 100 = £6 000

Total costs = Fixed costs + Variable costs
£20 000 + £1 000 = £21 000

Variable costs = Number of tables sold x Variable costs per unit
100 x 10 = £1000

Figure 2.12 Calculating break-even

Now test your understanding of how the break-even point is calculated by completing the activities below.

Activity

1 Copy and complete the table to calculate the break-even point of the various stationery items.

	Pens	Books	Pencils	Folder	Stapler
	£	£	£	£	£
Fixed costs	45 000	100 000	20 000	10 000	50 000
Price per unit	2.00	15.00	1.00	3.00	4.00
Variable costs per unit	0.50	7.00	0.20	1.00	1.50
Break-even point					

2 If the fixed costs were to increase by 10 per cent for all items, what do you think would happen to the break-even point?

3 Why might the fixed costs increase for a business?

Activity

A retro adventure gaming company is producing model kits of its characters for enthusiasts to purchase and make. The company wants to work out how many kits it needs to sell in order to set the sales team realistic targets.

- Fixed costs are £800 per month
- Variable costs are £4.00 per unit
- Selling price of each model kit will be £20.00
- The company estimate they will sell 150 kits per month.

1 Work out the company's break-even point by filling in the table below.

Number of kits	0	25	50	75	100	125	150
Fixed costs							
Variable costs							
Total costs							
Sales revenue							

2 Present the information in the table as a break-even graph.

3 Explain how you worked out the break-even point.

Activity

Revisit the example of Sarah and her ice lollies on pages 105–106

1 Calculate Sarah's fixed costs using the information on page 106.

2 Sarah charges £2.00 for an ice lolly, and her variable costs per lolly are 50p. Work out Sarah's break-even point per week.

Activity

Some businesses like to present break even in graphical form, known as a break-even graph. An example of a break-even graph is shown in Figure 1.10 on page 23.

Using the figures for Bailey Brown's garden chairs on the previous page, create a break-even graph that identifies the number of chairs Bailey needs to sell in order to break even (the break even point).

Stretch activity

Look again at the activity involving a company which plans to produce model kits of gaming characters.

1   The fixed costs increase by £100 each month. What effect will this have on the break-even point?

2   What should the company do to ensure its profit margins do not decrease with the increase in fixed costs?

3   What might be the effect of this action on the company? Explain your answer.

4.4 Identify the challenges when launching a new product

Risks

Launching a new product is an exciting as well as risky time for a business. This is because success cannot be guaranteed. Think about the process of producing a new product: the time developing the idea, the research, the costs involved in making it, etc. After all that investment, what if the product does not sell? It could spell disaster for a business. In 2015, *Management Today* reported that: 'Of 8560 product launches analysed by Nielsen, just 18 succeeded in becoming what it calls "breakthrough innovation winners". That is, achieving £10m of sales in their first year of trading and maintaining 90 per cent of that in their second.'

Read the following case study about a product that did not make it.

 **Case study**

A Wi-Fi connected cold-press juicing machine called 'Juicero' was produced in response to the increased trend for freshly-made juice from fruit and vegetables. The company secured around £92m in finance to design and produce the product which cost $399 in the USA. The juicer required users to purchase packets of diced fruits and vegetables which were plugged into the machine and transformed into juice. However, the business decided to shut down as they were unable to effectively manufacture and distribute the product. Sales were also disappointing, partly because consumers knew that the fruit and vegetables used could just as easily be squeezed by hand or even by an electric juicer.

Questions

1   What were the features of this product?

2   What do you think was the customer profile for this product?

3   Why do you think this product did not prove to be a success?

The main risks involved in launching a new product are described below.

Losing money

If a product that is launched does not sell at the expected level, money that has been invested by the business will be lost. If the business owner is a sole trader, he or she may have to sell their personal possessions to cover the debts incurred, because they will have unlimited liability.

Overspending the budget

If a business does not keep within the agreed budget and instead overspend on items that make the product, this will mean the business makes less profit per item. Think about the break-even figures that you worked out in the activities earlier in this section: if some of your costs increased because of overspending, then this would affect the number of products you would need to sell in order to break even.

Loss of investment

Often when starting a business or developing a product, you will need to seek investment so that you can purchase the items required to get started. You may approach a bank or ask family and friends for a loan. A bank will want to know about the potential business and will expect to see a business plan – a document that details information about the business, including costs and potential sales (see also Unit R064, page 54). The bank will then use this information to determine whether it will invest in your business by offering a business loan for a period of time. Friends and family that invest in your idea may, in return, be offered a share of the profits (assuming your business is a success and makes money). However, if your business does not succeed, the bank will still require you to repay the loan. Investors bank may have less confidence in you because your business history will not be positive and this could in turn make it difficult for you to obtain investment in the future.

Activity

The Museum of Failure exhibits failed products and services from around the world and opens for limited periods of time at locations including Toronto, Sweden, China and Germany.

Using the link **www.museumoffailure.se/**, research the types of design and innovation failures that can be seen in this museum. Produce a poster to advertise the museum, highlighting some of the products that can been seen.

Importance of customer demand for the product

Another challenge facing a new business is ensuring customer demand for the product continues, so that it will keep selling. Think about a simple and well-known product such as Kellogg's cornflakes. This product was first launched in 1906 and quickly became a firm favourite of customers, ensuring that demand has remained steady for many decades.

> **Activity**
>
> 1 Research the history of Kellogg's cornflakes and construct a timeline of most important dates for the product.
> 2 Research how the packaging of Kellogg's cornflakes has changed over the years using the following website: **www.kellogghistory.com/gallery.html** Write a summary of your findings.
> 3 Why do you think it is important for a successful business like Kellogg's to keep changing its cornflakes packaging and creating new advertisements for a product that has been successful for so many years? Explain your answer.

Importance of copyright

Every time you watch your favourite blogger online or a TV show, or listen to some music, you will be enjoying someone else's creative output. The person or organisation producing the creative content will own the copyright in their work. For example, J.K. Rowling owns the copyright for the character 'Harry Potter', as she created him and the world he inhabits.

Copyright materials take many forms, including illustrations, photos, sounds, music, recordings and literature. In the UK, copyright is protected by law. The Copyright, Designs and Patent Act 1988 details the rights of the copyright owner, as well as those who may want to use the product or work. If you own the copyright for a product or idea, it enables you to change the idea, share it, sell it or rent it, and prevent people from using it without your permission. Copyright is there to protect the owner's ideas. In the case of Harry Potter, this means that any company or person that wants to sell Harry Potter products, including books, films and merchandise, must obtain permission from J.K. Rowling to do so (and will most likely pay her a sizeable fee for the permission).

In order to obtain copyright status, your work must be:

- original – it must have been produced by you and be a new idea that has not been copied
- tangible – it has to be something physical, such as design drawing or the product itself. In the case of a song, this would by the song lyrics, as these can be seen.

Copyright is identified by the copyright sign ©. Any product or work displaying this symbol means it is copyrighted.

> **Activity**
>
> 1 Research some examples of copyright issues, for example, legal cases that have focused on copyright.
> 2 Share your findings with the rest of the class. Were you surprised by any of the examples given?

Importance of patenting

Patenting is slightly different to copyright. If a business patents a product it means they alone can legally produce and market the product for a set amount of time. This means the original inventor can take advantage of the hopefully increasing sales of the product before other companies are able to produce a version of the product that is similar, but not exactly the same.

Case study

Patents

Carlos Smith produced a home-made lemonade drink which his grandmother taught him how to make using a special family recipe. However, he had problems keeping the lemonade fresh using the materials that were available to him. Carlos developed a special type of bottle which would preserve the shelf life of the product. It involved a unique processing method prior to a new type of seal being placed on the bottles. This meant that the product did not need to be stored at a particularly cold temperature before the seal was broken. He is hoping that his Grandma's home-made lemonade can now be enjoyed by many more people.

Activity

1 Why might Carlos decide to patent the new type of bottle with the special seal for the lemonade?

2 How would having a patent help Carlos with this new technological design?

Trademark

A trademark is a mark that protects your unique brand from being copied by other businesses. It could be the name of your product or the service that you own. All trademarks have to be registered. Having a trademark means that you can put this symbol next to your brand name ®. If someone does try to use your trademarked product, you would be able to take legal action against them.

Why is it important to copyright and patent products?

Ensuring that you copyright and patent your product means others cannot produce a similar product without your permission. This means you can continue to produce and develop your product for the benefit of your business. You could, however, licence your idea, which would mean others can use your idea but they will need to pay for this privilege. This would be a source of income for your business.

Test your knowledge

1 Copy and complete the table below.

	Explanation of terms
Cost per unit	
Profit per unit	
Total costs	
Total profit	

2 Identify two examples of fixed costs and two examples of variable costs.

3 What are the main differences between psychological pricing and price skimming?

4 Write a definition of break-even.

5 How is break-even calculated?

6 How can break-even help a business?

7 Identify and explain two risks a new business will face when launching a new product.

8 Why is it important to know about copyright?

9 Write an explanation of a business patent. Give an example.

10 How does having a trademark help a business?

Read about it

www.bbc.co.uk/schools/gcsebitesize/business/
finance/accountingprinciplesrev1.shtml –
Explanation of revenue, cost and profit

www.accountingtools.com/articles/the-difference-
between-fixed-and-variable-costs.html – Explanation of the
difference between fixed and variable costs

www.tutor2u.net/business/reference/pricing-strategies-gcse –
Explanation of different pricing strategies

https://startups.co.uk/pricing-strategies-price-
skimming-penetration-pricing-and-premium-pricing/ –
Examples of how businesses use different pricing strategies

www.marketingdonut.co.uk/market-research/benchmarking/
choose-a-pricing-strategy – What to take into account when deciding
on a pricing strategy

www.bbc.co.uk/schools/gcsebitesize/business/finance/profitabilityrev1.shtml –
Revision guidance on breaking even

www.gov.uk/government/publications/copyright-acts-and-related-laws –
Text of the Copyright, Designs and Patents Act 1988

R066 Market and pitch a business proposal

About this unit

The aim of this unit is to develop the skills learnt in Unit R065, and to consider how a unique brand identity and promotional plan are important in business. This unit has different practical elements which will include how to plan, deliver and review a pitch.

Learning outcomes

LO1 Be able to develop a brand identity and promotional plan to target a customer profile

LO2 Be able to plan a pitch for a proposal

LO3 Be able to pitch a proposal to an audience

LO4 Be able to review the strengths and weaknesses of a proposal and pitch

How will I be assessed?

This unit is assessed by an assignment that will be set by the OCR examination board. You will complete this assignment individually and in your lessons at school. Your teachers will mark the work using the mark scheme.

LO1 Be able to develop a brand identity and promotional plan to target a customer profile

For this learning outcome, you will learn how important it is for a business to have a unique brand that customers can easily recognise, as well as the different methods that businesses use to promote their existing and/or new products to their customer profiles. You will use some of your existing knowledge from both Unit R064 Enterprise and marketing concepts and Unit R065 Design a business proposal.

Teaching content

In this learning outcome you will:

1.1 Build a brand identity

1.2 Plan brand ideas for a business challenge

1.3 Promote a product

1.1 Build a brand identity

What is a brand?

A **brand** is how a business can be identified. If a brand is successful, then customers learn to trust the brand and will purchase any new products produced under that brand. A brand is not just its name, but how customers regard the business as a whole. A brand can be recognised from a famous phrase, an image or a particular identity. Think about the task that you completed for the Getting Started activity: those brands are famous and most will have been around for several years or even decades.

So how does a business come up with a brand? Before a business can develop a brand, it will first need to consider the following elements:

- Strategy
- Brand personality
- Identity
- Image.

 Key terms

Brand How a business is identified by others, such as customers and competitors

Strategy

To stand out, a business needs to highlight its company purpose. A business will do this by focusing on its company values and messages, showing how these are different from those of other businesses. This will enable them to plan to develop products and/or services that are appropriate both now and into the future. These elements will form the strategy that a business uses to create its **brand image**. It is important that the business demonstrates its purpose and plans within their strategy so that they do stand out and are different from the competition.

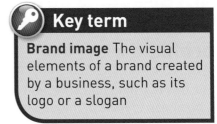

> ### Key term
>
> **Brand image** The visual elements of a brand created by a business, such as its logo or a slogan

Case study

Pret A Manger

The business Pret A Manger is well known for its commitment to the environment. The company wants to reduce waste, and as they make their food in kitchens either in or very near to Pret's shops on the day, any unsold food is given to homeless charities and shelters at the end of each day. By making this value clear as part of the brand, customers who are passionate about these values may choose to purchase food from Pret rather than another food outlet. This is part of Pret A Manger's brand strategy.

Brand personality

This refers to the techniques a business uses to present its ideas to customers. A company like Pepsi runs big-budget advertising campaigns that are bright and eye-catching and often feature famous personalities. By contrast, Dove promotes it body products by adopting soft, calming and soothing adverts. Dove are famous for promoting a caring, beautiful, thoughtful product and this is demonstrated by their brand. A brand personality can evolve over time and may even re-invent itself. In the same way that we can change the opinions and views that form our personality as we get older, companies may adopt a different approach as they mature. For example, Apple initially produced desktop computers but then, with the invention of the iPhone, iPod and iPad, it changed the way that technology is used in our modern lives. The company re-invented themselves and their brand. Some people are their brands – think of the famous company Virgin – its founder, Richard Branson *is* Virgin.

Activity

Research some of the businesses that Richard Branson has been involved with over the years.

1 Have you purchased any of his products/services? If yes, make a note of them.

2 How would you describe the personality of the brand, Virgin? Compare your answers with others in the class.

 ## Case study

Toys R Us

Toys R Us was first launched in England in 1985. At its peak, it was the toy store that all children wanted to visit to see the latest toys and spend their pocket money. However, in 2018, the last Toys R Us stores closed as the company went into administration. Toys R Us had not moved with the times and an increase in online purchases meant their huge stores were no longer relevant. Most stores were located in out-of-town retail parks

and, with cheaper online alternatives available to purchase toys, sales fell dramatically.

Questions

1 What was the brand personality of Toys R Us when it was popular?

2 What do you think that Toys R Us could have done to prevent the business closing?

3 Who has been affected by the closure of the Toys R Us stores?

Case study

Jamie Oliver Restaurant Group

Jamie Oliver has been in the public eye since his TV show, the *Naked Chef*, was first shown in 1999, going on to make several television series and write best-selling cookery books. His passion and enthusiasm for helping young people, through improvements to school meals, as well as setting up Fifteen, his restaurant venture to help young unemployed people back to work, has made him a popular personality.

As well as Fifteen, the Jamie Oliver Restaurant Group has a number of businesses including Jamie's Italian, Barbecoa and American diner-style restaurants.

Despite Jamie Oliver's popularity, in January 2018, Jamie's Italian closed 12 sites and asked for a cut in rent for its remaining sites. In February 2018, his Barbecoa restaurants went into administration.

So why is one of the UK's most famous and instantly recognisable chefs experiencing problems with his brand? Experts believe there are specific problems which could hinder a quick turnaround for his businesses. Questions have been asked as to whether the chef still feels the same passion for the Jamie's Italian brand, as he is now focused on his other ventures. Some believe those running the chain have tried to exploit the brand name without investing in it to keep it fresh and up-to-date, pointing out that the menu and décor of the chain have not changed since its launch.

Others believe that extremely high rents have been one of the biggest issues, pointing out that restaurants in areas such as Piccadilly and Bluewater shopping centre are among the sites that have closed. Jamie Oliver himself has blamed a 'perfect storm' of problems including high rents, increasing food costs and wages, the decline of the High Street and Brexit for the company's problems.

Questions

1 What are the main messages of this case study?
2 Research all the different products and services that are associated with Jamie Oliver. Are there any that surprise you, for example, because you did not know he was involved in that product or service?

Stretch activity

1 What do you mainly associate Jamie Oliver with?
2 What advice would you give to Jamie Oliver regarding his different restaurants?

Brand identity

Figure 3.1 on page 123 shows the six main elements of brand identity, as identified by Jean-Noel Kapferer, a branding specialist.

**KAPFERER'S
BRAND IDENTITY PRISM**

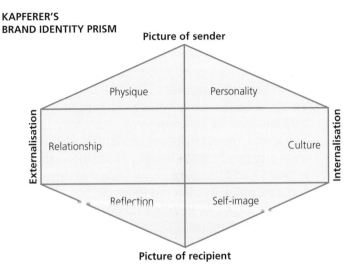

Figure 3.1 Kapferer's Brand Identity Prism

- **Personality** – brand personality is concerned with communication. It could be one person (for example, Richard Branson and Virgin), but generally it tends to refer to the features associated with the product, for example, the technology it uses.
- **Physique** – this is what the brand physically looks like, from the way that it feels when touched to the packaging of the product.
- **Culture** – the culture of a brand relates to how it is viewed by customers and potential customers. For example, a business that is discovered to be linked to organisations that sources cheap labour and provides inadequate working conditions will be exposed very quickly due to the increase in access to social media.
- **Relationship** – this refers to the involvement the brand has with its current and potential customers. It relates to the different methods a business uses to communicate with its customers and how successful it is at delivering good customer service.
- **Reflection** – this involves identifying the customer profile of the business. A business may produce a range of products ands so would have several customer profiles for the different products – for example, profiles for babies and young children, children, teenagers, adults and older people. Reflecting on this aspect of branding could result in customers potentially remianing loyal to the brand for many years.
- **Self-image** – this relates to how customers view themselves when using a company's product. If you know that your peers will make fun of you because you use a particular product, you are less likely to purchase it. However, if you purchase a desired product as soon as it is launched, your peers may be very impressed and regard you positively.

Case study

In 2013, the eight-storey commercial building, Rana Plaza, collapsed in Bangladesh, killing more than 1,100 workers. The building contained five clothing factories, whose workers produced garments for 23 different famous brands, including Primark. The owners of the building were criticised for the working conditions the workers had to endure. For a period of time, this negative publicity affected Primark, too. However, since the disaster, Primark has continued to support the families affected by the disaster and they have implemented changes to the manufacturing of clothes that are sold in the UK.

Another form of brand identify is the way it looks visually. This includes consideration of colours, design, typeface and logo placement.

- Companies will use a logo that visually impacts on a customer. Think about products produced by popular brands such as Apple, Microsoft, BMW, Johnson & Johnson, Nerf and Sony – they all have a specific business logo that forms part of their identity. The logo may always be positioned on a particular part of the product – for example, Cadbury always have the name 'Cadbury' on each square or piece of their famous milk chocolate bar.

- As well as a logo, the business may only use a particular colour or font (typeface) for the text that describes the product or service. Using the example of Cadbury again, the colour purple and the swirly writing make their Dairy Milk Bar an instantly-recognisable brand.

- A company can become famous because of the unique design of its product. Toblerone, for example, is a triangular shape. There is no other bar like it which makes it unique and its design has become part of its identity.

Activity

Your school has a brand identity.

1   Think about all the different elements of your school's brand identity that enable people who are not involved in the school to identify with it. Note these down.

   a   Look at your school's website. What are the different visual elements of the website? Focus on the way the website looks, the links, font and colour of text, etc. Make notes of your research.

   b   Describe the different elements of the school's brand identity that appear on its website.

2   Draft an email to your head teacher suggesting improvements that could be made to the school's brand identity, including the school website.

Activity

Research the Rana Plaza disaster, including Primark's involvement in it. List the actions Primark has now implemented to improve its business culture as a result of this terrible event.

Activity

Identify a famous brand name you are familiar with. Use the 'Brand Identity Prism' to write about how the six different elements of the prism relate to your chosen brand.

Case study

Skoda

For many years, the car company, Skoda, was ridiculed by the motoring industry for producing cars that people did not want. Then Skoda was taken over by Volkswagen (VW), which paved the way for changes: new designs were introduced and the cars became more reliable, modern and relevant. This in turn led to happy customers and a successful and profitable company.

Question

What conclusions can you draw about successful re-branding from this case study about Skoda?

Brand image

Brand image can include the visual elements of a logo, but there is more to an image than just a symbol, sign or logo, as explained below.

- Quality – brand image involves quality. If you purchase a product and it breaks within the first week, your view of the company may change. If you take the product back and exchange it for the same model and then it breaks again, would you take it back and replace it for a third time or ask for a refund? A business does not want to gain a reputation for producing poor quality goods or providing poor service, as customers will make their views known. People often post a review of items or the company itself on the business's website or by rating products online. Online reviews can therefore be a good gauge as to whether or not a product you are thinking of buying is a quality item.

- Low cost – this is also a factor in creating an image for a brand. Most customers want 'value for money' – that is, they want to feel the amount of money they paid for the item reflects its actual worth. However, sometimes customers are happy to spend a little more if they feel this means they will get a better quality product. Indeed, some brands are built on this image – John Lewis states it is 'Never knowingly undersold', and pledges that if you find the same product cheaper elsewhere it will refund you the difference.

- Lifestyle – this is another aspect of brand image. Particular products and services are aimed at a certain lifestyle based on **customer profiles**. So, for example, people who like skiing will want to know about the latest ski equipment and accessories because they enjoy this particular activity, whereas someone who plays golf would not be as interested in ski-themed goods. Knowing the lifestyles of your customers is important and will enhance your brand image too.

- Customers' perceptions – these are the views customers have of your business. These will vary depending on their experience of being your customer. This is why it is so important to ensure that all employees treat customers well, so they remain loyal to the brand and continue to provide repeat custom.

Key term

Customer profile
Researching vital information about customers to ensure that products and services appeal to them

Activity

Ryanair operates a budget airline that flies all over Europe and aims to provide excellent value for money. However, the company does still receive complaints from its customers. Furthermore, the owner, Michael O'Leary, is a controversial figure, especially with regard to his comments about Ryanair's brand image.

1 Research the Ryanair business. Find some recent articles that feature both positive and negative elements of this controversial business and identify the main points in each.

2 Use your research findings to create a blog about Ryanair and customers' perception of the business.

Why businesses use branding

Reputation and trust

Branding is important to a business, as it forms an important part of the business's reputation. If you have a good reputation, customers will talk about you in a positive way to others, which might make them purchase one of your products or services. However, if your reputation is negative, this may put off potential customers, which will ultimately mean that you lose customers, leading to a reduction in profits. Some business reputations can be damaged by one single event. A company can spend a great deal of time and money on re-building a damaged brand. Sometimes this works, but often it does not.

Case study

Read the following case studies which look at the reputations of three different businesses.

Case study 1

In 2018, BMW was forced to recall more than 300,000 cars in the UK because it had been reported that the engines in some cars were cutting out due to an electrical fault. They contacted customers who had purchased specific cars between March 2007 and August 2011. An investigation by the BBC's 'Watchdog' highlighted several customers whose BMW car engine cut out while driving. BMW was also criticised for failing to tell the Driver and Vehicle Standards Agency of the electrical failure in its cars between 2011 and 2014, as it was required to do so.

Case study 2

A report issued by a group of MPs has told the government that the company, Whirlpool, should be made to recall millions of tumble dryers because of the number of fires that have been started by their products. More than 750 fires have been started in homes in the UK since 2004 because the fluff from the drying process has made contact with the heating element and has then caught fire. The risk appears to be with older dryers and, since November 2015, the company has contacted nearly 4 million potentially affected customers and offered them a choice of having their appliance replaced or repaired. However, many customers are still concerned about whether their dryer is a fire hazard. MPs therefore want the government to help to ensure that customers are safe and protected.

Case study 3

Perrier is famous for its sparkling water, but in 1990, impurities were discovered in some bottles. The impurity was a toxic substance called benzene. Within one week of the findings, the company decided to recall 160 million bottles of the water. The company subsequently discovered that the toxic substance was caused by human error due to filters that had not been changed at the bottling plant. Move forward to 2018, Perrier is now available in 140 countries around the world and sells over one billion bottles in a year.

Questions

1 Identify the main points made in the three different case studies.
2 Building customer trust is another reason why a brand is important to a business. Using the points you have identified, state whether you would trust these brands? Discuss your reasons as a class.

Recognition and image

Famous brands are recognised in various forms, whether by name, logo, type of font used on the product or colour. Having a clear brand means loyal customers are easily able to identify the brand and will continue to buy the brand's products or services because of the trust they have placed in the brand.

Many brand images are quite simple and yet have a strong presence, which is why a simple and bold design may be the most easily recognised by consumers.

Activity

1 Identify the following famous brands.

2 What do these brands have in common?
3 Create a picture quiz of a variety of different brands that people should recognise. Aim for a minimum of ten brands. Make sure the images you choose do not show the name of the brand.

Quality

When you purchase a product or service, you do not expect it to break or stop working as soon as you get it home. Sometimes consumers think that spending more money will ensure a more superior product. But is it always worth spending more money? Think about some of the brands you have read about in this chapter. Do you associate any of those brands with quality?

Businesses want to produce good quality products and services every time, so that customers make repeat purchases. Poor quality products will have to be discarded or altered, which will cost the business materials and time. Businesses invest money to ensure that their products and services are the same quality each time they are manufactured. Businesses also strive to achieve quality standards, which means they are able to prove to specific organisations that their products or services are worthy of the specific standards.

Examples of quality standards include:

● BSI Kitemark – you will probably be familiar with this mark (see Figure 3.2) as it appears on many different products and services. It is a quality mark owned and operated by the BSI (British Standards Institution), and is one of the most recognised symbols of quality and safety.

Figure 3.2 BSI Kitemark

- ISO 9000 – this quality standard is set by the International Organization for Standardization (ISO) and it require a business to ensure its products and services fully meet quality and safety standards. The ISO 9000 standard looks specifically at business's quality management systems and encourages them to constantly improve these. An example of the type of logo that a company that complies with ISO 9000 might display is shown in Figure 3.3.

Price can also influence customers to purchase a product, because they may feel it reflects the status or quality that the product or service has within the market. For example, the fashion store, Miss Selfridge, sells its own interpretation of the 'Knife boot' for £35, which is over £600 less than the Balenciaga original priced at £645 (see Figure 3.4). Le Specs sunglasses (see Figure 3.5) are a status product, with various models priced from £40 to £80, while similar versions produced by Topshop cost around £25.

Figure 3.3 Balenciaga knife boot

Activity

1 What are your initial thoughts about the alternatively priced products above?
2 Do you like designer brands in general? Justify your answer.
3 Would you consider purchasing a cheaper version of a famous brand?

Discuss your answers with others in your class.

Differentiation

The products that were highlighted such as the boots from Miss Selfridge and Balenciaga enable consumers who might like these products to afford them even if they have very different incomes. They offer two different options: the designer pair and the high street pair. Some people will only settle for the designer pair, but the majority of consumers are unlikely to spend £645 on a pair of boots. This is known as differentiation – giving people the opportunity to purchase a product, which is little different from the original, at a price point to suit their income. For example, KitKat produce a number of alternatives to the original two-fingered bar. These include KitKat with four fingers, KitKat Chunky, KitKat bitesize, white chocolate KitKat as well as a range of different flavoured KitKats.

Figure 3.4 Le Specs sunglasses

Activity

Think of five products that have been produced with similar alternatives. List the alternatives.

Adding value

A successful brand image can add value to its products. Think about when you have purchased some biscuits in a supermarket. Have you noticed that the supermarket's own versions of the products are very near to the branded version of the product? Would you purchase the known brand, which is probably more expensive, or the supermarket own brand, which may be considerably cheaper? It comes down to personal preference, of course, but this highlights the importance and power of a brand.

Case study

Supermarkets profit by selling standard own-label products that are identical to their 'value' brands

An investigation has discovered that many supermarkets are selling standard own-label products that are identical to their value range. Investigators looked at the ingredients and nutritional values of a number of products across the two price tiers – standard and value – and concluded that in many cases there was almost no appreciable difference between the two. In some cases, the two versions of the product were even produced in the same factory. The only difference between the two versions was their packaging and, of course, the higher price being charged for the standard range.

The investigators looked at a range of products, including cheddar cheese, corned beef, UHT milk and clear honey. Price variations between the budget and standard versions of the identical products ranged from 25p to 50p per product – which may not sound much but could make a significant difference to the weekly shopping bill.

Questions

1   What are your thoughts about this investigation into brands?

2   Are there certain products that you think do taste differently to own supermarket brands? Would you swap?

Make some notes then discuss with the class whether you think this will affect the products that you will purchase in the future, and why.

Build customer loyalty

Having a successful and reliable brand helps a business to increase loyal customers. For example, you may have a particular type of shampoo or toothpaste that you always buy; if this is the case, then you are loyal to that brand and will be regarded as a loyal customer. Many businesses want to increase the amount of loyal customers they have, but this is hard to do, especially when people want value for money. Yet some brands cost much more than similar alternatives and this does impact on customer loyalty. In the past, people would be more loyal to a particular branded product, but with the increase of value products in shops, customer loyalty is decreasing and can be difficult to maintain for a business. However, some businesses continue to enjoy a very loyal following – a good example of this is Apple.

Customer loyalty can also be measured by the service that a customer receives when purchasing a product or service. Many businesses undertake surveys to measure customer satisfaction. If a problem occurs with a product, consumers want to know that a business will deal with them in a professional way to ensure they remain loyal and likely to make future purchases.

Case study

Customer service

A poll by *Which?* magazine looked into which UK brands offered the best customer service. The poll found that First Direct, Lakeland and Lush were the highest scoring brands for customer service in the UK in 2017. Members of the public were asked to rate 100 of the biggest brands and the online bank, First Direct, was rated highest with 63% of the respondents to the poll saying that its staff's attitude was excellent. The lowest rated brand was Sports Direct, which received low scores in the poll for resolving complaints and staff being unhelpful.

Question

What does this case study suggest about the importance of good customer service?

Branding methods and techniques

Logos

Earlier in the unit we looked at a variety of different logos for famous brands, including Nike, Pepsi and Lloyds Bank. A logo is used to help customers identify a business easily by a symbol, picture or font that represents the business. The purpose of the logo is not normally to show what the business sells, it is purely for identification and helps to increase customer loyalty. Logos are rarely redesigned after they have been created, as this could cause confusion for customers.

There are three main types of logos, as described in Table 3.1.

Table 3.1 Types of logos

Type of logo	Explanation	Example
Ideograph	Image that has no specific association with the company	Starbucks two-tailed mermaid
Pictographs	A simple picture, such as an symbol or an image	Nike tick
Logotypes	A particular font or letters representing the business	Coca-Cola

Activity

Research and identify two examples of each of the different types of logos described: ideographs, pictographs and logotypes.

Sounds and jingles

The power of a brand to captivate can be found not only in an image but also in a particular sound or jingle from an advertisement. You can find these on the internet in the form of blogs or adverts within the blog, pop-up adverts on social media or other platforms, or more traditional methods such as on the television or radio. Examples of how a business can use music, sounds or jingles to sell products that are related to their brand include the 'holidays are coming' words sung as part of the Coca-Cola Christmas advert and 'I'm lovin' it' from McDonalds. Some of these sounds and jingles can also be linked to business straplines or catchphrases and slogans.

Straplines, catchphrases and slogans

A strapline is a few words that are related to the business such as Nike's 'Just do it'. This will appear at the bottom of an advertisement in some form, demonstrating the business's values and personality. As a business who makes and sells sports products, a simple strapline of 'Just do it' tells Nike's customers in three words what they are about, informing them to 'Just do it'.

A catchphrase is slightly different to a strapline as it is a sentence or phrase which is repeated by many people over a period of time. Some people or characters from movies are famous for having a catchphrase that identifies them. Examples include 'Do, or do not. There is no try' – Yoda from *Star Wars: The Empire Strikes Back* or 'You're fired' – Lord Sugar from the TV series, *The Apprentice*. This is the same as a business having a catchphrase to help advertise its product or service. An example is 'They're not Terry's, they're mine', for Terry's Chocolate Orange.

A slogan is a series of words which always appears within an advertisement and, like a catchphrase, will form part of the product or service over a long period of time. An example is 'The first vacuum cleaner that doesn't lose suction', from Dyson.

Activity

Supermarket advertising often focuses on quality and price. Many of their slogans are quite similar.

Can you identify the supermarkets by their advertising slogans shown below?

Slogan	Supermarket
'Live well for less'	
'Save money live better'	
'Every little helps'	
'Big on quality, [?] on price'	

Celebrity endorsements

For years, businesses have used famous celebrities to advertise their products and services in the hope that customers will purchase them. The famous person is paid to have their name associated with the brand, so it is important that the celebrity represents the business in the way that they want. There have been examples over the years of celebrities who have been 'dropped' by a business because of the way they have conducted themselves. The businesses do not want their brand image damaged by the actions of their celebrity endorsers. An example of this is the Brazilian footballer, Ronaldinho. He was axed by Coca-Cola after appearing with a can of Pepsi during a press conference in 2012. Losing his contract with Coca-Cola was rumoured to have cost the footballer up to $1 million in lost earnings.

Many famous people are also asked to use their celebrity status to increase awareness of charities. The involvement of famous people to promote a particular cause can mean that people who may not normally give money to charity will do so because of the celebrity's association. Look at the Children's Society website to see the celebrities who are ambassadors for the charity: **www.childrenssociety.org.uk/about-us/our-organisation/ charity-ambassadors**

Characters

Characters are often used to advertise products that will appeal to children. Remember Tony the Tiger from Kellogg's Frosties or the Honey Monster from Sugar Puffs? These are products that are aimed at children and by creating a cartoon character with a slogan together with appealing advertisements, many generations of children have persuaded their parents to purchase these products. Tony the Tiger was created in 1951 and over the years his image has changed very little (see Figures 3.5 and 3.6).

Figure 3.5 Kellogg's Frosties – advertising from 1950s

Figure 3.6 Kellogg's Frosties – current advertising

1.2 Plan brand ideas for a business challenge

Assess the appeal to the customer profile

Unit R065 Design a business proposal focused on identifying customer profiles for a product (see Section 1.1, page 73). Remember that customer profiling is when a business uses its knowledge and research into customers to segment them in order to build up an image or profile of their ideal customers.

A customer profile involves producing a description of an 'ideal' customer, that details where they are likely to live, what they do for a job, how old they are, what they like to buy and how much they probably earn, etc. The business then uses this information to target its products at these customers. Having this information is vital, as it enables the business to plan its brand ideas to ensure that it appeals to these customers. For example, if a new yogurt for children was to be produced, it would have to appeal to both the child and parents because they will be purchasing the product. Today, consumers are very conscious about processed food and especially the sugar content of products aimed at children, so this might be something that a business would highlight within its branding.

Activity

1 Think about the customer profile of each of products shown below and complete the table with your notes.

Product	Who are its main customers?	Customer profile of person who will purchase the product

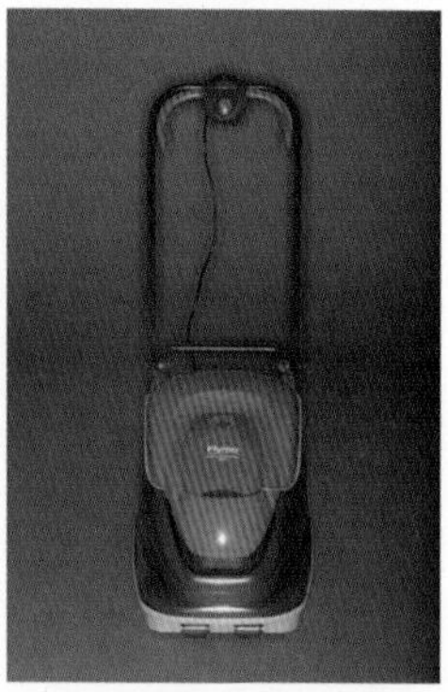		

2 Compare your answers with another person in the class. As a pair, discuss why you think these three different products would appeal to the customer profile you have chosen.

3 Research the advertising of similar products to those shown above and make notes of the different methods of advertising these brands use. This could include type of advertising, different sales techniques such as '3 for 2' and celebrity endorsements. Share your findings with the rest of your class to find any similarities or differences. Are you surprised by any of the results?

Research other brands

It is important that the brand appeals to its audience, so businesses will try to make sure that their products are different to others in the consumer market in order to generate sales. A business will design a product that is different by first researching the market to see what already exists.

Figure 3.7 Selection of chocolate bars

Strengths and weaknesses

Figure 3.8 shows a chocolate counter within a supermarket with brands including Hershey, M&M's, Dairy Milk, Kinder and KitKat. All of them are different. A business that wants to sell a new chocolate bar will need to research the market to find out the competition. Businesses will analyse this competition, by looking at the strengths and weaknesses of the different products, as this will help them create something different.

Unique selling point (USP)

Businesses will always highlight the strengths of their products, as this helps with customer sales. All businesses try to find a major strength of their product, which they can refer to as its unique selling point (USP). Making sure that your product 'stands out' above others is the key to making a sale. We are all individuals and we all have different tastes, so what appeals to you may not appeal to someone else. That is why businesses need to know what their customers will purchase, which relates to customer profiling. USPs of products or services may include the quality of the materials used to make it, the selling price, the varieties of colour or where it can be bought.

Formulate brand designs for a proposal

There is a lot of coverage in the media regarding ingredients used in the food and drinks that we consume, and recently this has focused heavily on sugar. Sugar can be found in many products including some that you would not expect, such as pasta and curry sauces, which are categorised as savoury food items. Sugar can be used to prolong the shelf life of a product, which is important to food producers as they want their products to be safe to eat for a long period of time.

If a company decides to design and produce a new drink in what is an already competitive market, one of its many considerations might be the sugar content of the new product. The company may decide the product should have a long shelf life as well as be a healthy option for consumers. When formulating the brand design, the company would need to put these overall aims into its proposal so that they can be achieved.

 Case study

The celebrity chef, Jamie Oliver, has been highlighting sugar within his campaigns over the years, which have mainly focused on sugary drinks. In April 2018, the UK government introduced a sugar tax. This means that companies who produce sugary drinks are now charged a tax according to the total amount of sugar in their products, although fruit juices and high-milk content drinks are currently exempt.

The new tax has resulted in some manufacturers reducing the sugar content of their drinks, for example, Ribena, Fanta and Lucozade. The introduction of this tax has led to a price increase for some of the most sugary drinks, but the government has estimated that the tax will generate over £500 million pounds, which it will use to help fund sports in primary schools to help tackle childhood obesity.

Relate to research findings for other brands

In Unit R065, the importance of research when considering a new business proposal was demonstrated. For a business, being clear on what competitors currently offer can enable them to identify gaps in the market which new product idea could fill. If the product is successful, others may copy the idea, but the business will have potentially been the first one to produce such a product. A business might choose to develop a product after completing primary and secondary research.

For example, washing powder used to be placed in a drawer in the washing machine. Following research into consumer habits and opinions, washing liquid was developed. Both products were still placed in the machine drawer, however. Further research was then conducted which indicated that people would like to avoid the mess of placing the product in the drawer and so washing tabs were developed, which are placed directly inside the washing machine drum. All three products are still available and do the same thing, but the product has evolved as a result of continued market research. Any research that a business completes must relate to the area of the market that they are entering and be able to provide the business with the necessary findings to help develop a product.

Activity

Using the information in the case study, research how brands within the food industry have had to change as a result of the sugar tax. You might consider branded products such as baked beans, tomato ketchup, cereals and jam.

Assess the likelihood of success or failure of different options

You have already looked at how a business will assess the strengths and weaknesses of competitors' products, which helps it focus on the individual USPs related to its product. This assessment can also be used on any new product designs for a business as well as existing products that have been re-developed. A business must assess its own designs to ensure that they will appeal to the known customer profile. The results of this analysis will help a business predict whether the product is likely to be a success or failure, although no one can know for sure until the product goes on sale. Ensuring that a thorough assessment is completed will give the business its best chance of success.

Examples of business successes

The popular television programme, *Dragons' Den*, has enabled many products and services to be produced. Sometimes the Dragons invested, but sometimes they did not. Here are some products that you may have heard of.

- The 'Tangle Teezer' featured on *Dragons' Den* but failed to get any investment. Despite this, when the programme was aired, the company website crashed because of the interest and demand for the product. It is now stocked in shops worldwide, has won many awards and generated millions of pounds worth of sales.

- The popular children's travel suitcase known as 'Trunki' can be found in many airports around the world. The inventor rejected an offer of a 50 per cent share of the business from a Dragon. The Trunki is sold around the world, including John Lewis in the UK. It has gained many awards, enabled the product portfolio of the brand 'Trunki' to be expanded and made the company millions of pounds.

- The most well-known product from *Dragons' Den* is Levi Roots' Reggae Reggae Sauce. He accepted an initial investment from some of the Dragons. The brand of Levi Roots has continued to expand year on year, and now includes meal kits, drinks, table sauces, seasoning and even cookery books.

Examples of business failures

There are some businesses that clearly did not research the market well, as their products failed. Failure of a product often means the company has not assessed the market properly. The case study below highlights how even a well-known company can sometimes get it wrong.

Activity

Using the information in the Dasani case study, compose an email to a design assistant that highlights the importance of thorough research before launching a new product. Give them some hints and tips of good practice and examples of how this could be used to develop a new product design.

 Case study

In 1999, Coca-Cola launched Dasani water in the USA. It was a huge success and so in 2004, the Dasani brand was launched in the UK. However, it soon became known that what was advertised as purified water was in fact tap water from Kent which had been remineralised. Once the national press found out, news spread quickly. This was followed by a batch of the bottled water becoming contaminated and as a result the company withdrew all 500 000 water bottles that were in circulation. Within five weeks of its launch, Dasani was no more.

1.3 Promote a product

When a product is going to be advertised there are a number of different elements that a business should consider. These include promotional objectives and the methods of promotion that could be used.

Promotional objectives

Promotional objectives are the targets that a business wants to achieve as a result of the promotions used to advertise a product. These targets or objectives are described below.

To raise awareness of the product or service

Selecting the right method of promotion to inform customers about a product is very important. If people are not aware of the product's existence, sales will not be generated. Raising awareness can take many different forms, for example, new food and drinks products are often available to taste within a chain of supermarkets to generate an interest from consumers. Equally, pop-up stands could be placed within city centres to enable consumers to try the products.

To remind

Coca-Cola was invented in the late nineteenth century and continues to be one of the most famous brands in the world. Yet, the company still continue to advertise and produce new products. This ensures that customers are still aware of the company's products. Look at the Coca-Cola website to see their range of products: **www.cocacola.co.uk/en/home/#**

To differentiate

Businesses differentiate their products from those of their competitors so that consumers will purchase their products instead of their rivals. Differentiation can be achieved through branding, packaging, performance or design. Think about the impact of Microsoft and Apple on technology and how these businesses continue to influence our lives.

To persuade or inform

When products are produced, unless they are totally unique and different, the promotional methods selected by the business must try to persuade or inform consumers to buy the product. Think about the shampoo market. They all do the same thing, which is to clean our hair, but companies have to persuade us to purchase their product rather than another. They will do this by choosing a promotion or highlighting features that are likely to be appealing to the target consumer.

To create market presence

Breaking into a new market and trying to create market presence is both an exciting and daunting prospect for any business, but once met, it is a real achievement. There are many different forms that a business can use these days to create a market presence. For example, social media can have a positive and instant effect on a product or service. Equally, this can also be a negative effect if the experience for consumers is not positive and this is shared or reviewed using a social media platform. Creating a 'buzz' for a new product or service will help create market presence.

To boost market share

In order for a business to boost its market share, it must already be known within the market. Market share is measured by looking at a specific market as a whole, such as the fizzy drinks market, and calculating the total sales from the main competitive brands. The graph in Figure 3.8 shows the 'leading soft drink brands ranked by convenience sales value in the United Kingdom in 2017'. This gives an indication of the market share of particular products within one market.

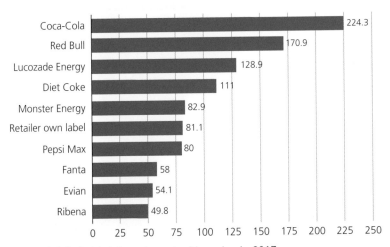

Coca-Cola	224.3
Red Bull	170.9
Lucozade Energy	128.9
Diet Coke	111
Monster Energy	82.9
Retailer own label	81.1
Pepsi Max	80
Fanta	58
Evian	54.1
Ribena	49.8

Figure 3.8 Soft drink brands ranked by sales in 2017

Methods of promotion – digital promotion

Promotion has dramatically changed over the past ten years with the introduction of digital methods to promote products. Each day we are exposed to different forms of advertising as soon as we use a technology product.

Online advertising

A business might set up their own website to promote their business. This website may include some online advertising; this can be as simple as a web page that promotes the products or services that a business sells, or it could be adverts known as '**pop-ups**' thatappear onscreen when we are looking at a website. These pop-ups draw our attention away for a few seconds from what we are looking at with the hope that we will then pursue the advert further. Websites may also contain **banner advertisements** at the bottom of a page or a strapline which changes frequently. These are popular within news websites as the news is updated on a regular basis.

Social media platforms

These target particular products to the user. Information such as age and location are stored within the personal information section of the user profile. If you visit a new town or city, your social media

Key terms

Promotion The different methods used by a business to ensure that customers are aware of its products and services

Pop-ups Mini adverts that appear on screen to temporarily distract the audience and draw them away from what they are looking at, before disappearing

Banner advertising A form of advertising containing product or service information that moves across a screen platform will often know where you are and target advertising related to that location directly to you. Social media platforms include Instagram, Twitter, Facebook and LinkedIn. When you update your status, this gives the platform even more information which can be used for promotional methods.

Promotional emails

These are another form of digital promotion that businesses may use. For example, Amazon may send you emails based on previous purchases that you have made or searches that you have completed. These emails could contain special offers such as free delivery, discount codes or vouchers. This is a form of **direct marketing**, meaning that it is targeted at specific customers. These emails can be stopped by the consumer by unsubscribing to cancel further communication.

SMS texts

A business may choose to use this type of promotion to promote a brand. This form of promotion will mainly be used by your mobile telephone provider. Like emails, these adverts can be stopped if you text the business directly.

Podcasts and blogs/vlogs

Podcasts, blogs and vlogs are digital platforms that can be accessed at the user's convenience.

- **Podcasting** – this is a recording of one person or more discussing a specific topic. They can be in an audio or video format which is then downloaded. The number of downloads can be easily measured which can help determine the popularity of a podcast. Podcasts tend to be produced on a regular basis so it is important that you don't disappoint your audience by forgetting to post a new one. Large businesses will often sponsor podcasts in return for an advertisement or promotion of their product during the podcast.

- **Blog** – this is a written form of information where the author (known as a blogger) writes on topics that interest them and their followers. It is important for businesses purposes that you research your topics correctly and post your blog on a regular basis to keep the interest high for your followers. Particularly influential bloggers are often paid to promote or endorse products because companies know that if they are seen to use a product, those reading the blog will be tempted to go out and purchase the product too. This is a form of advertising.

- **Vlog** – this is very similar to a blog, except that it is a visual form of information that you can post for your followers. Once your vlog is well known, your followers could have the option to subscribe to a specific channel, where more vlogs can be accessed specifically for these subscribers. As with bloggers, vloggers can promote certain products or services within their communications as a form of promotion. Businesses are often willing to pay huge sums of money for the vlogger to promote their products or services and hopefully boost sales.

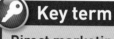

Key term

Direct marketing A method of advertising that is targeted at specific customers

Activity

1 In pairs, discuss who is your current favourite vlogger or blogger that you access on a regular basis. Has this changed in the past two years? Discuss your answers.

2 Does your favourite vlogger or blogger promote products or services? If so, which ones? Have you ever bought any of the products or services that they are promoting? Discuss your answers.

3 Research the top five podcasts, bloggers and vloggers of the current year. Do any of these surprise you? Share your answers with the rest of the class.

Stretch activity

Write a guide that explains how you can start to produce a blog or a vlog for a person who is not aware of this form of promotion.

Methods of promotion – offline/traditional promotion

Offline or traditional forms of advertising, such as leaflets or flyers that are put through the front doors of houses are still an accessible form of promotion for businesses.

Flyers and leaflets

People often hand out flyers to consumers in the street that advertise products and services. It is a cheap method of advertising and one that can reach many different potential customers, but the risk is that they will end up in the recycling bin. Leaflets can also be inserted within magazines or newspapers. This was a very popular form of advertising, particularly in weekend newspapers, but due to the rise in printing costs and increased awareness of the environmental impact of using paper, fewer leaflets are now produced. As Christmas approaches, large stores such Marks and Spencer and Debenhams will often distribute a gift guide in a newspaper to advertise their products.

Figure 3.9 Flyers

Advertisements

Advertisements that are shown on the television or in a cinema are seen by large numbers of people. Businesses pay to have advertisements shown at specific times when audiences are large to gain maximum publicity. With different forms of viewing available to consumers because of digital platforms, the ability to download programmes on tablets, laptops, mobile telephone etc., advertisements can now be targeted to viewers who are attracted to a specific type of programme. The Christmas advertising campaigns by large businesses such as John Lewis and Marks and Spencer create lots of positive publicity and their adverts will appeal to many consumers. Other forms of advertising that businesses use include:

● **Newspaper advertisement** – depending on the size of the advert, this is a costly method. Other factors include whether the advert is in black and white or full colour, the day that the advert appears and even the page which it appears on. So, a quarter of a front page, colour advert at the weekend will cost more than a small black and white advert in the middle of the newspaper on a Wednesday. Advertising in national newspapers which have a circulation of the whole of the UK will be much more expensive than advertising in a local newspaper with a limited readership.

- **Magazines and journals** – this is another popular place in which to advertise. Magazines tend to be produced weekly, fortnightly or monthly and are usually aimed at readers in a specific market – e.g. fashion, home, football, cars or technology to name a few. Journals often relate to specific job sectors, such as science, catering, education or marketing. Advertisements that appear in magazines and journals will be specific to a particular interest or target market. For example, a technology magazine will contain articles about the latest technology and gadgets and the advertisements will often be related to this subject. There may be special offers for certain technological products. A journal about catering will feature reports relating to the hospitality industry and will have advertisements that will be of interest to the target market of the journal.

- **Cinema advertising** – this is still a popular form of advertising as businesses know they can reach a large audience, particularly when a film is first launched. The advertising will be targeted at a specific age range according to the film certificate being shown, so for a family film an advertisement for Center Parcs may be shown, whereas a film with an 18 certificate may advertise alcohol. The high costs of producing an advert that will appeal in a cinema setting and the popularity of the film being shown will influence businesses when planning their advertising budget.

- **DVD advertising** – this is now going out of fashion as the DVD market is declining as a result of the popularity of online streaming services. In its prime, advertising was a part of the DVD experience and producers of the product made it difficult for users to forward the adverts. This was a tactic to ensure that users had to watch the adverts rather than skip them. Businesses would pay large amounts to have their adverts at the start of this feature.

Figure 3.10 Modern billboard advertising

- **Billboards** – these have changed as a result of digital influences. Although the traditional methods of a very large poster being placed on a large display board on the side of a building or bus shelter can still be seen, increasingly, digital billboards are appearing. Digital billboards are also known as out-of-home (OOH) advertising. The advantages of this form of advertising are that it is affordable, as the business will save money on printing costs as everything is created electronically and sent electronically to the locations of the billboards. There is no time wasted waiting for printing, as once the advert is sent, it can be uploaded quickly for the duration of the promotion period. Adverts can also be displayed at certain times of the day, which can be beneficial to certain types of business. For example, if you are offering a breakfast service, adverts can be shown at the start of a day to try to entice customers to your business.

- **Direct mail** – a form of advertising that is targeted specifically at consumers. Mail is sent to a person which features special offers relating to a product or service that they have used in the past. This may include vouchers to spend, information regarding a new offer or special codes to gain 10 per cent off or free delivery on items that are purchased within a specific time frame.

- **Buses and taxis** – vehicles are a useful form of advertising for businesses as they move around a city or a town each day. The advertisements are on the side and back of the vehicle and will be seen by many people in one day. Advertisements on buses can also be put over the windows as they use special materials so that customers can still see out of the windows. Schools and colleges often use buses to promote themselves.

- **Commercial and digital radio stations** – use advertising each day as they provide a source of income for the radio station. Some adverts will be local to the area where people will be listening, while others will be for nationally-known businesses. Businesses will pay more money to advertise at peak times of the day but this means their advert will achieve the maximum impact on the audience – for example, more people will listen to a breakfast show than a show on at 9.00 p.m. in the evening.

Events

- **Festivals** – these have enjoyed a revival over the past few years. Many festivals are no longer just about music, now you can go to food festivals and car festivals. Festivals can be a good form of promotion, as they provide an opportunity to sell goods at an event for a period of 3–4 days. Special promotions can be used to try to get customers to buy your products. The key is to make sure that you have enough stock so that you don't run out on the first day!

- **Trade fairs and shows** – these events appeal to people who have a similar interest, for example, the Education Show will attract teachers and lecturers and will often feature different speakers who have specific knowledge that the event attendees will be interested to hear. At a trade fair there will also be the opportunity to promote products and services related to those who work in the trade.

Activity

Research past John Lewis and Marks and Spencer Christmas advertising campaigns. Note down the year of the advert and describe what you see. Why do you think these adverts appeal to a wide range of people?

Figure 3.11 Advertising at a festival

- **Customer VIP events and brand launch** – these are organised by large organisations as a 'thank you' to customers for investing or purchasing large amounts of their products or service. These events often have very large budgets but the business putting on the event can use this as an opportunity to advertise their products or services in the hope that the guests will continue to be loyal to the company. Businesses sometimes use brand launches or customer VIP events to promote their latest or newest products. This can be a great method of promotion, especially if it appears on social media with updates being created by people attending the event.

Sponsorship

Sponsorship is another traditional method of promotion that has been used for many years to promote a business's brand. Examples include, placing the name of a business on a sports team's shirts or sponsoring a large community event. By sponsoring an event, the business's name will be displayed on merchandise associated with the event or mentioned by a presenter covering the event. Television programmes can also be sponsored by a brand, meaning that any advertisement breaks will feature the brand's products.

Figure 3.12 Sport sponsorship

Product placement is when a product is featured on screen, usually in a film. The product will be placed in a particular scene, which the camera will focus on. Businesses pay the film company to have their products featured within the film. James Bond films are famous for including product placement – some of the brands that appeared in the 2015 film *Spectre* included Gillette, Range Rover, Aston Martin, Arsenal Firearms and Heineken.

Select and justify appropriate promotional methods

Key factors that influence the selection of methods

Businesses need to select the most appropriate methods to promote their business, by considering a number of different factors.

- **Objectives** – a business will need to decide what it wants to achieve by the promotional method selected. Does it want to gain new customers? Remind customers that the product is still available? Persuade customers to purchase its product rather a competitor's? How will it promote its USP?
- **Budget** – if you are a small business with a limited budget, then initially you may need to select a method of promotion that does not cost too much money, such as leaflets or flyers. However, this will limit your promotion to local customers.
- **Time** – this refers to the time that it will take to design your method of promotion. If a leaflet is to be designed, who will do this? Who will print it? Will you use the office printer or a professional company that specialises in printing? If you are recording a radio advertisement, a script will need to be written and the advert recorded and edited. Likewise, if a television advert is being produced this will take time to produce as you will

need to consider where it will be filmed and who will be involved. All these different considerations will need to be built into a timeline. For example, if you know you have six weeks to produce and record a TV advert, a timeline will need to be devised for each stage of the production, such as booking the film crew and editing the film, so that it is produced on time.

● **Research** – researching any events you may want to attend is a good idea to see if your products would sell at such an event. Does your product meet the target audience of the event or exhibition? Equally, if you are looking to sponsor an event, would your business be relevant and therefore benefit from this form of promotion? It is important to research your market.

● **Booking** – if you are going to attend an event or exhibition to sell your products, you will need to be organised and contact the event organiser, pay a deposit and ensure that you or whoever is attending the event is available. You will also need to ensure that you can produce enough stock to sell at the event as you don't want to run out! Equally, you don't want to have stock left over if at all possible.

Appeal to customer profile
You have already seen how newspapers, magazines and trade journals attract readers and how this can determine the type of advertising that is produced for the customer profile. For example, if you are planning to organise a coach holiday for people aged 60 years and over, you will need to design leaflets/brochures or send out direct mail to those customers who form your customer profile. If this information is incorrect, then the costs involved in producing these advertisements will be wasted. If a special family pass is being offered for a famous city centre attraction at a reduced price, advertising on a commercial radio station during the breakfast show would reach a wide audience. It is important that the type of advertising selected for the advertisement must appeal to the target market to generate the required sales.

How different methods complement each other
Your business may want to use a variety of different methods of promotion that complement each other over a period of time. This means combining promotions. Think about how McDonald's promote their products compared to B&Q or Macmillan Cancer Support. These organisations all have a different approach to marketing and will use several different methods to inform others of their products or services. Having a promotional strategy is important for a business, so it is essential that it is well planned so that time, money and energy is not wasted. For example, McDonalds will produce advertisements on both the television and radio when they launch a new menu for the summer or winter season. They may also offer discount vouchers in national newspapers at the same time, which people can use for a limited time. Having a variety of different promotions at the same time can maximise the impact of new deals offered by a business.

Activity

Research the different methods of promotion used by Lidl, Amazon and Boots the Chemist.

1 Describe the methods used by each company.

2 Are their promotions all aimed at the same type of customer or do they vary the method depending on the target audience?

3 Do you think that the methods of promotions used by each company complement each other? Explain your answer.

Test your knowledge

1 Write a definition of a brand.

2 Why is a brand important to a business?

3 What is the difference between a brand personality and a brand image?

4 How can a brand add value to products? Explain your answer.

5 What is the Brand Identity Prism?

6 Why is a logo an important aspect of a brand?

7 What is the difference between a slogan and a strapline?

8 Identify three celebrities who have endorsed different products. Name both the product and the celebrity.

9 What does USP mean?

10 Why do businesses set themselves promotional objectives?

11 Identify seven different forms of promotion that a business may choose to promote its products.

Read about it

www.thebrandingjournal.com/2015/10/what-is-branding-definition/ – Explaining what branding is.

www.bbc.co.uk/schools/gcsebitesize/business/marketing/brandingandpackagingrev1.shtml – Revision guidance looking at what a product is

www.tutor2u.net/business/reference/brands-and-branding-introduction – Introduction to brands and branding

www.marketingdonut.co.uk/marketing-strategy/branding/ten-ways-to-build-a-brand-for-your-small-business - tips on building a brand

www.coca-cola.co.uk/stories/coca-cola-one-brand-marketing-strategy – Coca Cola explain their marketing strategy

www.americanexpress.com/us/small-business/openforum/articles/5-steps-to-determine-your-unique-selling-point/ – Advice on finding a business's USP

www.marketingdonut.co.uk/marketing-strategy/branding/developing-your-usp-a-step-by-step-guide – How to further develop your USP

www.digitaldoughnut.com/articles/2016/july/digital-marketing-vs-traditional-marketing – Pros and cons of traditional and digital marketing methods

LO2 Be able to plan a pitch for a proposal

This learning outcome focuses on the skills that are required in order to plan and inform others about a business proposal. One method used is pitching, and this learning outcome focuses on the aims and how to 'pitch' business ideas. Businesses use a vast array of different resources which are useful and enable them to prepare for any questions that may be asked by potential investors.

Teaching content

In this learning outcome you will:

2.1 Plan a pitch

2.1 Plan a pitch

A **pitch** is a short communication that tells an audience about a business proposal with the objective of trying to gain support for the idea. Entrepreneurs often use this method to communicate their ideas to people who may want to invest some money into the business. If a person invests in a business, the entrepreneur accepts a loan of money from the **investor** and in return, the investor will receive some of the profits as a reward for their investment. The number of people who watch the pitch will be limited. Figure 3.13 shows how a pitch works.

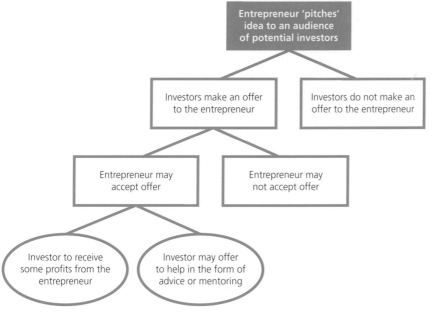

Figure 3.13 Process of making a pitch

Consider audience

Needs/interests – when a business plans a pitch, it is a good idea to research who the potential audience will be. For example, the business could find out more about the audience's business background, organisations they have worked with before and their hobbies and

Getting started

A pitch is a way of communicating a business proposal to an audience. In pairs, create a mind map that details the different skills and information you think you will need to deliver a successful pitch.

Activity

A presentation is different to a pitch. In pairs, research the main differences between a pitch and a presentation and summarise these. You could also use your experiences of delivering a presentation or pitching an idea.

Key terms

Pitch A method of communicating and presenting a business proposal to an audience

Investor A wealthy individual listening to a pitch who may loan money to a business to help get it started in return for a share of the profits

interests. The more information the business has, the better! The pitch can then be developed and altered to consider the needs and interests of the audience who hopefully will then be interested to hear more.

Accessibility of content – if a business knows more about their potential audience, they can then tailor the pitch to include specific points that may appeal to the potential investors. If they know, for example, that the audience will be quite young, then the language used may be different to that used with an older audience. It is important that any person delivering a pitch is always prepared to explain any jargon or specialist terms that relate to the product or service. No matter who the audience is, the person delivering the pitch must understand all its elements, as they could be asked specific questions and the answers must be well informed.

Convincing others of the likely success – a business must appear confident in the information that they are giving, be professional in their approach and above all, be enthusiastic about the business proposal. If a business appears unconvinced by their own business idea, why would others want to invest?

Using all these different elements will hopefully convince the audience that the business proposal would be successful and that they should invest.

Objectives of the pitch

When planning a pitch, a business must establish early on what it is they are trying to achieve. The overall aim may be to communicate a message to an audience, but how this message is given will be determined by the objectives that the business sets itself. Objectives are the different steps taken to enable the business to communicate the message or pitch, as explained below.

To inform

This is the business's chance to explain the proposal to the audience, which could include what the product looks like, how it will be promoted, how much it will cost to produce and what the break-even point is.

To persuade

The audience of potential investors need to be convinced that the idea is going to work. They may have to listen to several pitches in one day, so the pitch must stand out from the rest so that the audience really hear what is being said. Think about reality television shows like *Britain's Got Talent* or *X Factor*. The judges have to listen to many different people performing and make a judgement within a short amount of time. With these shows, if a performance is different and unique then it is more likely to get through to the next round. This is the same for any business pitch. If a slightly different pitch is planned and the business 'wows' the audience with the product, finance details and business sense, this could result in them wanting to invest in the business idea. The business needs to persuade the audience using the presenter's personality, skills and business knowledge.

Timeframes

The timing of the pitch is important. Normally a business will be told of the time allocated to speak to the audience and the potential investors may also want to ask some questions about the business proposal. These will be asked after the pitch time is completed. It is therefore important that the pitch is practised so that it is delivered within the timeframe that the business is given.

Communicate effectively

When communicating with any audience it is important to establish a 'presence' with the audience and engage them into the presenter's way of thinking. This can be done by pacing how the pitch is presented. If the presenter speaks too quickly it could mean that the audience may not be able to understand what is being said. Speaking too quietly means that the audience may not hear what is being said. Vital parts of information could be missed by the audience which could impact on the outcome of the pitch. A presenter may be nervous, which the audience will understand, and nerves can make the presenter act in a different way, but if the pitch has been practised and it is clear the presenter knows what he or she is going to say, this will help the presenter deliver a successful pitch.

Venue

If the business is able to select the venue where the pitch will take place, it is important that the location is convenient for the audience to reach. If the audience have a difficult journey to find the venue, they may arrive feeling unsettled and less inclined to listen to a pitch. Making sure that the room is the right size is important – a room that is too big may make the presenter appear 'lost' in the space; equally if the room is too small, there may not be enough space for everyone who wants to watch the pitch.

A business should check beforehand that the room layout is appropriate for the pitch. Again, if the room is too small, it may not be possible to move furniture around in the way that suits the audience. A presenter may need some props or accessories that form part of the pitch and a lack of space may mean that these props cannot be displayed properly. A business should try to view the room in advance – drawing a sketch of how the room should look could help the presenter when planning the pitch.

The presenter will need to consider whether they will need access to a laptop or projector, etc. Equipment may need to be booked in advance at the venue, unless the presenter plans to bring their own equipment with them. The business should make sure time is left to set up the equipment and upload any visual aids that may be on a memory stick. It is vital that they check the equipment is working properly before the pitch begins, because equipment failure could have a huge impact on the success of the pitch.

Figure 3.14 Planning and preparation is the key to success

Identify appropriate media

When completing any communication in front of an audience, the presenter may want to have some pre-prepared resources to help deliver their message.

Some typical resources are:

PowerPoint presentations

PowerPoint presentations can be prepared in advance and contain information on different slides, which the presenter can then communicate with the audience. Using presentation software means the business can design the slides exactly how they want in terms of background colours, font colour, type of text and inclusion of images and graphs. Different images can be highlighted to make them stand out at certain points during the communication, for example, by focusing on different parts of a graph. PowerPoint also enables a business to set up the timing of the slides which may help the user when delivering a pitch. Setting up timings is a useful feature as it can enable the presenter to concentrate on the content of what they are saying rather than having to use a mouse to 'click' onto the next piece of text, image or slide. This could improve the message that is being delivered to the audience.

Handouts

Information that is relevant to a pitch could be handed out to the audience as handouts or leaflets. The presenter can then specifically refer to these during the presentation and they form part of the message being communicated to the audience. Providing each audience member with a handout about the product provides the presenter with an opportunity to discuss the contents of the leaflet as part of the pitch.

Verbal prompts

When planning a pitch some people find it useful to have access to notes or prompts that remind them about the order of what they need to say whilst completing the pitch. There is often a lot of information that needs to be communicated, so having some form of notes can help the presenter make sure they do not miss out any vital information. Imagine if the presenter forgot to tell the audience how much the product costs but told them the break-even point. However, it is important that the presenter does not read from a script when delivering a pitch to an audience. If they read something out, it means that the presenter will not be interacting with the potential investors by demonstrating eye contact and confidence. Reading a script will not demonstrate pitching skills, but having notes which can be referred to is acceptable.

Figure 3.15 Think carefully about the structure of your pitch

Structure of a pitch

We have established that it is important to prepare for a pitch in terms of knowing the audience, working out the overall objectives, considering the venue and whether any prompts will be required. Having considered these important aspects, developing the overall structure of how the pitch will be delivered will ensure that all the information will be communicated to the audience.

A structure for a pitch will normally contain an introduction, main content and a conclusion. Remember that a pitch is generally quite short so when a business plans a pitch pitch, the structure should be kept simple.

Activity

1 Think of a lesson that you have recently completed in school that you enjoyed. Write down why you enjoyed the lesson. Was it because of the different activities that you had to complete or because of the equipment you were using?

2 Thinking about this lesson, write down the different stages of learning. How did the teacher deliver the main content of the lesson? Did he or she do something that was a little different to normal?

3 Share your findings with the rest of the class. How could you use these findings to help you structure a pitch?

Introduction

The presenter should introduce themselves to the audience so that they know who the presenter is. The presenter should inform the audience of the business proposal clearly. If the presenter can demonstrate confidence this in turn will give them confidence to continue with the pitch. The presenter should stand up straight, make eye contact with the audience, speak clearly and smile. A smile will mean that the audience will smile back.

Main content and visual aids

After the presenter has introduced themselves and the business proposal, it is important that they work through the different parts of the pitch in a logical order, ensuring that nothing is missed out. Pausing briefly between the different sections that have been planned will show control. Using prompts such as handouts, leaflets, visual aids, etc. will help this process. This is when time spent practising the pitch will pay off, as the presenter will know what to say and is less likely to stumble over their words. Remember the presenter must not read a script. This is the moment that could make a difference to the business – it is *their* moment and the audience will want them to do well. The business must demonstrate all the hard work that has been put into this pitch.

Conclusion

This part of the pitch gives the presenter the opportunity to sum up the main points of the business proposal including the product, customer profile, price, marketing plan, costings and where it could be sold. This information will have already been given in detail, so this is just a quick reminder for the audience. If the presenter makes the conclusion stand out in some way, this could be the point at which potential investors decide to invest. For example, the pitch could end with a famous quote, tell a relevant story or with a challenge for the audience. Finally, the presenter should thank the audience for listening and then invite some questions.

Anticipate potential questions

By inviting questions, the presenter gives investors the opportunity to find out more about what they have just heard. Once a pitch is planned, it is a good idea for a business to try and anticipate some questions that they might be asked. For example, a pitch may describe the market research that was completed. An investor may want to ask why a questionnaire was used instead of another form of primary research. Another question might be based on the selling price, such as 'Why are you charging £7.99 for the product?' Planning answers to these types of questions helps the presenter keep calm and answer the questions confidently, which will give a positive impression to the audience. Saying nothing is never a good idea.

What to wear

It is important to look professional when delivering a pitch. Dressing appropriately can also give the presenter confidence to perform well during the pitch. The presenter should plan what they will wear and make sure that it is clean and pressed ready for the day. Getting a good night's sleep the night before is also important so that the presenter is refreshed for the morning. Eating a good breakfast on the morning of the pitch will help the presenter be ready for the day.

Test your knowledge

1 When planning a pitch what should a business think about?
2 Why should a pitched be planned?
3 Explain what is meant by 'Objectives of a pitch'.
4 Give two examples of visual aids that could be used within a business pitch.
5 Why is personal appearance important when pitching to an audience?
6 How should a pitch be structured?
7 Why are questions asked as part of a pitch?

Read about it

www.startupdonut.co.uk/sales-and-marketing/sales-techniques/preparing-your-sales-pitch-checklist – Tips on preparing a sales pitch

www.bbc.co.uk/schools/gcsebitesize/business/marketing/productlifecyclerev1.shtml – The different methods of creating customer awareness

https://simplicable.com/new/promotional-objectives – The different objectives you may have when promoting a product

www.skillsyouneed.com/ps/personal-presentation.html – Tips on presentation, with links to more in-depth guidance

www.mindtools.com/pages/article/elevator-pitch.htm – Guidance on how to prepare an elevator pitch

https://openclassrooms.com/en/courses/2901541-launch-your-innovative-venture/4282256-the-structure-of-a-pitch – Advice on preparing a pitch

LO3 Be able to pitch a proposal to an audience

For this learning outcome, you will learn how to present to an audience and develop your personal skills to successfully deliver a professional pitch. You will also consider the importance of supporting others such as your peers and how practice can positively influence how you deliver and perform a professional pitch.

Teaching content

In this learning outcome you will:

3.1 Use and develop personal and presentation skills to deliver a professional pitch

3.2 Support peers

3.3 Review a practice pitch in order to plan for a professional pitch to an external audience

3.4 Deliver a professional pitch to an external audience

Getting started

Individually write down what you think might be the main differences between verbal skills and non-verbal skills. Write down some examples of each type of skills.

3.1 Use and develop personal and presentation skills to deliver a professional pitch

Personal presentation

When completing any kind of interview, presentation or pitch in a business setting, it is important that you create the right impression. You want to show your best attributes and demonstrate that you have taken the time to present yourself in the best way. This suggests to the audience that you are serious about this potential opportunity. For more on how to dress for a presentation, see Section 2.1 What to wear on page 152. Good personal hygiene is essential and will give you confidence. Being prepared with the resources required for your pitch will give the impression that you are organised. This can also calm any nerves, as being prepared shows that you care about what you are about to explain to your audience.

Activity

Think about the different clothes and accessories that you own. Copy and complete the table by listing which of these items would create a professional image for a business and which are only suitable for casual wear.

Suitable for business	Suitable for casual wear

Professionalism

When you visit any organisation, your first impressions of it are often influenced by the staff that you come into contact with. Creating a positive first impression is important as customers' opinion of the business may be influenced by this first interaction. For example, if you arrive at a business and the person at the reception desk is chewing gum, looking at a mobile phone and is unaware of you waiting, your impression of the business will probably be negative. If a shop assistant is rude to you when you make a purchase, you will probably not be keen to return to that shop again in the near future. Displaying **professionalism** when delivering your pitch will encourage potential investors to listen to what you say and take you seriously.

Verbal skills

Much of our communication with others involves using our **verbal skills**. Demonstrating professional verbal skills will enable you to:

- provide information, for example, pitching an idea to an audience
- issue instructions to colleagues, for example, how to operate machinery
- make requests or confirm arrangements, for example, confirming a meeting.

There is more to verbal skills than simply opening your mouth and speaking, as outlined below.

Clarity

The clarity of your voice refers to how clearly you speak to the individual or audience to convey your message. This is important as if a speaker cannot speak clearly, then they will not be able to explain the information that they are trying to get across to an individual or audience. Speaking clearly, exaggerating words and having confidence will enable a person's voice to be heard.

Did you know that practising tongue twisters can help voice clarity? Practise saying 'red lorry, yellow lorry' over and over again. Or you could try saying 'you know New York, you need New York, you know you need unique New York.'

Tone

The tone of your voice is about how you portray the information that you are giving. If you are angry, the tone of your voice will demonstrate this. Equally, if you are smiling, this affects the tone of your voice in a positive way. You can often tell if someone is smiling while speaking on the telephone, even if you cannot see them.

Voice projection

If you are nervous, you may speak quietly, making it difficult to be heard. If you shout, this can put a strain on your voice, so it is important that you learn how to project your voice in a way

Key terms

Professionalism
Consistently displaying appearance and conduct of the highest quality and is associated with the impression that is given to others when working in a business

Verbal skills Using the voice to communicate with others in such a way that they understand the message that is being conveyed

Activity

Identify the main attributes that are needed by a member of staff to create a good impression in a business situation. Share your thoughts with the rest of the class.

that is comfortable for you to maintain throughout any verbal communication and which your audience will enjoy listening to. Getting your voice projection right can be achieved by practice.

Top tip! The best and simplest way to practise projecting your voice is to stand at one end of a room and ask a friend or family member to stand at the other end and listen to you speaking. They can then advise you whether or not your voice can be heard clearly. Practice will help you learn how much you need to project your voice.

Use of language

Formal language can be defined as language that is less personal and uses a variety of rich and stimulating words to describe what the person wants to express. It may also include technical terms and jargon specific to the subject being discussed. **Informal language** is the type used in conversation with family and friends, perhaps including slang words or abbreviations that you would not use in formal language. For example, how you speak to your friends will be different to how you address your teachers or some family members. The language that you use may differ, for example, when speaking to children, we usually speak in a slightly different way and use clear and simple language so that they understand us. We often alter the language we use according to the requirements of the situation. In a business setting you will need to demonstrate your ability to use formal language, as this will create the right impression for the business.

Persuasiveness

This is a verbal skill and it refers to presenting information in such a way that it will be positively received and will help you achieve what you want. When pitching to an audience, you will hope to persuade one or more people to support your business proposal. By communicating the positive aspects of a business plan as well as all the required information to make a decision, you will enable potential investors or interested parties to decide if they want to support your business venture.

Key terms

Formal language Less personal language that is used in business and other professional settings, that often features a variety of words, including technical terms and jargon

Informal language Language that is used in conversation with friends and family and which may include slang or abbreviated words

Activity

Using the knowledge you have gained about verbal skills, copy and complete the table to identify and describe a situation where you have demonstrated each of the skills shown.

Verbal skills	Description of situation
Clarity	
Tone of voice	
Voice projection	
Formal language	
Informal language	
Persuasiveness	

Non-verbal communication

In the 1970s, Albert Mehrabain was responsible for creating a communication model which suggested that only 7 per cent of what is communicated by humans is verbal, 38 per cent of communication is by the tone and volume of our voices and 55 per cent is through non-verbal methods, such as body language, eye contact and gestures.

Non-verbal communication includes the following:

Body language

This is a very important aspect of communication and can be defined as the way that a person delivers a message using their body. Our bodies communicate our feelings, emotions, health and status, sometimes without us even realising it. If you are feeling vulnerable, you might try to make yourself look physically smaller to 'hide'. If you are bored while trying to communicate a message, this can make others feel the same way.

Communication model

- Verbal
- Non verbal
- Tone and volume

7%

38%

55%

Figure 3.16 Mehrabain's communication model

Activity

Look at the facial expressions shown in the images and write down what you think this indicates they are feeling.

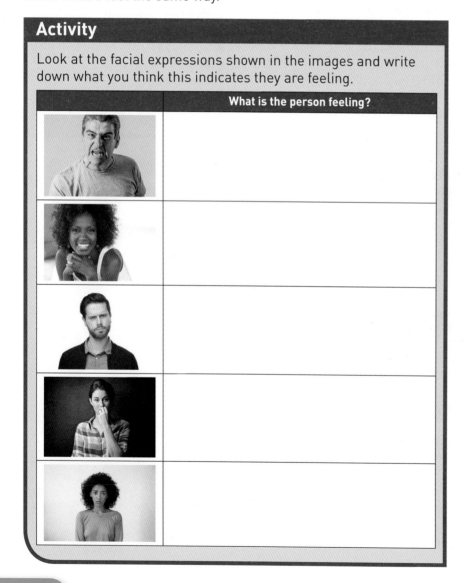

	What is the person feeling?

Posture

How you stand or sit will engage the person or audience that you are communicating with, which will impact on the message that you are trying to communicate. If you sit up straight or stand tall, this can give the impression that you are feeling confident and in control. If your shoulders are rounded and you are sitting slouched, you will appear uninterested and your audience may find they feel the same. Sitting with your arms folded can appear defensive, whereas leaning towards shows that you are interested in what they are saying.

Eye contact

Looking a person in the eye while you are talking to them and maintaining eye contact shows that you are interested in what they are saying. If you look away or over their shoulder, it indicates that you are disinterested or bored by what they are saying. Not maintaining eye contact is also a sign of embarrassment or nervousness.

Gestures

Gestures are a form of signalling to a person to inform them of how we are feeling. Examples of gestures that we demonstrate could be a wave to say hello or goodbye or a handshake. Other examples are shrugging our shoulders to inform someone that we are not sure, nodding or shaking our heads or maybe fiddling with our fingers because of nerves.

Facial expression

Our facial expression will often demonstrate how we are feeling. If someone tells us something that is a great surprise, our face will show this feeling. If we receive sad news, it is difficult not to show this by our expression. Facial expression is therefore an important aspect of non-verbal communication.

Confidence

Confidence can be displayed by our facial expressions, gestures, posture and body language. Look at the image below which shows several different individuals. All look confident in their own way. They may have different facial expressions, be displaying different body language and have different postures and gestures, but all do display some form of confidence. Appearing to be confident gives others an idea of how you will react in different situations that you may face.

Figure 3.17 Confidence can be shown in many different ways

> ### Activity
>
> In pairs, discuss how you think that a confident person will behave when first meeting a person. Draw a flow diagram to illustrate your discussion.

Use of notes/cues

When delivering a pitch, some people find it useful to have notes or prompts to remind them of the order of what they need to say and to help them remain focused. Lots of information needs to be communicated to your audience, so having notes can ensure you do not miss out anything that is vital. Cue cards are another type of prompt. These are small pieces of card or paper that easily fit into the palm of your hand which contain words to prompt important information. Imagine if you forgot to tell the audience how much your product costs but told them the break-even point. It would not make any sense!

As mentioned in Section 2.1 of this unit (page 150), never read from a script when making a pitch, as you will not be able to maintain eye contact with your audience and they will have less confidence in you and your business. Referring to notes or cue cards, however, is acceptable and will help you remain focused.

You may like to number or clip your cue cards or notes together in the corner in case you drop them because of nerves – this will ensure you can easily reorder them and carry on with your pitch.

Use of appropriate visual aids/media

Visual aids can give a person presenting a pitch the confidence to deliver a good presentation. Visual aids draw the audience's attention away from the presenter while the aids are being explained, which can be helpful as continually being gazed at by an audience can be intimidating. However, the visual aids must be relevant to the message that is being communicated. (See Section 2.1 (page 151) for more on how to use visual aids in a pitch.)

Activity

Produce a handout for someone planning to make a pitch to an audience, which provides hints and tips on the importance of verbal and non-verbal skills and personal and professional presentation skills.

Self-confidence, enthusiasm, self-belief

When we are young, we often listen to and believe what others say about us which can damage our confidence. How many times have you thought, 'I can't do that' or been told by others that you won't be able to achieve your goals? This is wrong. The famous author J.K. Rowling, who wrote the *Harry Potter* series of books, was rejected by several publishers before someone finally believed that her writing would be successful. She did not give up and instead demonstrated persistence because she knew that her creative work was good enough to be published. Having self-confidence means thinking and believing 'I can do this'. Sometimes, we have to train our minds to think differently, a process referred to as changing you 'mindset'.

Another example of self-belief and confidence is clearly demonstrated by the business Gandy's (see Unit R065, page 97). The owners of the business wanted to make a difference and their brand is now very successful, but they had many knock-backs before their flip flops eventually began selling.

These two examples highlight how self-belief is an important aspect within business and this can also be demonstrated when communicating with an audience in a pitch. If you have self-belief that your idea will work because of your extensive research and planning, this will be demonstrated during your pitch.

Activity

In 1984, Richard Saul Wurman had an idea to hold a conference to discuss how Technology, Entertainment and Design (TED) converged. This led to the development of TED talks, which today are accessed and shown around the world each day via the internet. According to its website (**www.ted.com**), TED is about 'the inspired format, the breadth of content, the commitment to seek out the most interesting people on Earth and let them communicate their passion.'

TED talks are no longer than 18 minutes in length because they believe that this is the perfect amount of time for a presenter to inform and hold the attention of an audience.

Research and listen to some TED talks on the following topics:

- self confidence
- self-belief
- enthusiasm.

Make notes on the main messages of each talk and feed back your findings to the rest of the class.

Target the needs and desires of the audience

Understanding your audience when pitching your business proposal is key to achieving success. An awareness of the organisations that the audience members represent will help you understand their expectations. For example, if most of the audience are entrepreneurs who own their own businesses, they will understand how this opportunity can impact on the future of your business proposal. A business may understand the risk element of investing in a new business idea, because money will be lost if the business fails. Having a mixture of business expertise within the audience is the ideal situation because it maximises your opportunity to gain an investor. After all, you only need one person to decide that your proposal will satisfy their business needs and desires.

Case study

Take control and learn how to make a great business pitch that will impress your investors

Pitching to investors can be one of the toughest things you have to do when running a business.

With so much depending on a successful outcome, learning to control your nerves can make the difference between a lacklustre performance and getting the investment you are looking for.

Follow these steps to make sure you give a memorable business pitch – for all the right reasons!

Step 1 – Know your audience

- Understand what a potential investor is looking for and then adapt your pitch accordingly. This means doing your research.
- Look online at who will be part of the audience and the type of businesses they have been involved in. What experience or interests do they have? Can you use this information to make your pitch more appealing to your audience? Showing that you've done your homework will impress potential investors.
- Clearly showing that your business can attract and retain customers is vital to a prospective investor, so make sure you inspire confidence by having relevant facts to hand: Why will customers choose your business? How big and how profitable is the potential market? What do you offer that your competitors don't? These are key points that you must include in your pitch.

Step 2 – Use 'memory palaces'

- Going blank on stage during a pitch is perhaps an entrepreneur's worst nightmare! People who regularly rely on reciting facts from memory often use a method called 'memory palaces'.
- Here's how it works: pick a place you know really well, perhaps your house. Now try linking your presentation with the various rooms and objects in your house. Do this chronologically, so that as you mentally approach the front door you start your introduction, before moving into the living room where you see a photograph of your family, reminding you of the market for your product, then into the conservatory where you see a telescope that reminds you of your company's outlook or vision. Clearly this method only works when it is adapted to suit your own personal circumstances, but the basic principle is pretty simple.

Step 3 – Practice and then practice again!

- Despite all their preparation and research many business owners forget to practise delivering their pitch beforehand. This is essential if you are going to beat those nerves when you are on stage.
- Practice your pitch until you are entirely comfortable with it – this could be as many as six times – and ask someone to give you feedback on its content, flow and pace. Familiarity with your pitch will ensure it sounds polished and professional.
- Practice delivering your pitch in front of an audience – this could be your colleagues, family or friends. If you belong to a business club, this may offer an opportunity to practise delivering your pitch to business professionals.

Step 4 – Nerves are normal!

- It is completely normal to feel anxious before making a pitch and no amount of practice can get rid of pre-pitch nerves entirely.
- Try to turn your nervousness into something positive – feeling anxious is a sign of just how much this pitch means to you and your business, so use it to communicate your passion for your product.
- Prospective investors will want to hear you speak with passion – a person who is entirely without nerves in front of an audience is likely to give a dry pitch that will impress no one.

Question

Read again the article on tips for making a business pitch and make a check list of the main points.

Time management

Using your time effectively is important, so decide the most important elements of information that you want to get across to your audience. Don't run over your allocated time as you may have to leave out important information and risk not providing enough details of the business proposal.

Rehearse in advance of a pitch and deliver a practice pitch

For any important communication in front of an audience, it is vital that you rehearse and practise a pitch or presentation. The TED talks that you viewed for the activity above will have been written and rehearsed by the presenters to get the information across to their audience. Practising your pitch will show you whether you are trying to get across too much or too little information, and you may need to alter it slightly so that you make good use of your allocated time.

Answer questions from the audience

It is a good idea to try and anticipate some questions that you might be asked as a result of the information the audience hear during the pitch. Anticipating the type of questions potential investors might ask will enable you to prepare some answers. For more on answering questions from the audience, see Section 2.1 (page 151–2).

> **Activity**
>
> In pairs, discuss the advantages and disadvantages of practising something. It could be practising for an examination, speech, concert, presentation or debate. Using the information from this discussion, individually create a leaflet that highlights the importance of practising for a presentation or pitch.

> **Activity**
>
> Refer back to the article about overcoming nerves during a pitch and the topics covered in Learning Outcome 3. In pairs, create a three-minute pitch about a new healthy drink aimed at children. You need to quickly come up with the following:
> - A name for your drink.
> - What age of child it is aimed at.
> - How much the drink will cost.
> - Where it can be purchased.
> - When it will be available.
> - A simple logo for the drink.
>
> You only have 30 minutes to complete this activity, including time to practise the pitch. Your teacher will not be expecting perfection as you only have a short time to complete this task, but make sure that all the bullet points above are covered. You will deliver your pitch to two other groups who will have the opportunity to comment on your pitch.

Activity

Working in pairs, listen to another group's pitch and then give feedback to the group. To help you prepare your feedback, note down your responses to the questions below as you listen.

Once completed, share your feedback with your peers.

1 Name of group members.
2 What is the name of the drink?
3 Who is the drink aimed at?
4 What is the cost of the drink?
5 Where will the drink be available for purchase?
6 When is the drink going to be available?
7 What did you think of the logo design?
8 How did the presenters come across to you? Confident? Nervous?
9 Were the presenters organised?
10 Did you have the opportunity to ask questions?
11 How were the questions answered?
12 Sum up your overall impression of the pitch.

3.2 Support peers

In business, there are many different ways that people support each other with their work. This will also happen in your school or college by supporting your own peers in different lessons or with different situations that may occur. If a business is preparing for a meeting, an event or a pitch, colleagues will often help to show their support. Supporting others is important as you never know when you might want someone else's help!

Give and respond to constructive peer feedback

Constructive feedback is a way of giving your opinion of a presentation or a pitch made to you. The constructive element of the feedback requires you to make polite suggestions as to how the pitch or presentation could be improved. The person who receives the feedback can then use these comments to improve their pitch.

Feedback sandwich

One way of giving constructive feedback is the **feedback sandwich** (see Figure 3.18). The two slices of bread represent positive feedback with the filling of the sandwich being made up of constructive criticism. As someone delivering a feedback sandwich, you begin with positive comments, then constructive criticism and then end with another aspect which is positive. The idea is that the person receives more positive comments than negative comments. The receiver then acts on the constructive comments to improve and refine their pitch.

Key terms

Constructive feedback
Giving your opinion of something (both positive and negative) and suggesting ways in which improvements could be made

Feedback sandwich
Three different parts of constructive feedback – the two slices of bread represent positive feedback with the filling of the sandwich being made up of constructive criticism

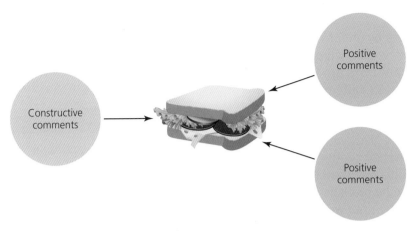

Figure 3.18 The feedback sandwich

Here is an example of a feedback sandwich:

Part 1 (positive): 'Your business proposal idea is really original, and I think will definitely appeal to your target market.'

Part 2 (constructive): 'With regard to the poster that you designed as part of your advertising campaign, I found parts of it difficult to read. This could have been because of the font you used or the use of yellow.'

Part 3 (positive): 'The knowledge and understanding of break-even was really great and your enthusiasm for your proposal was really clear throughout the pitch. Well done.'

Phrasing feedback constructively

It can be difficult to be told something negative, so you must be sensitive of the person's feelings. Choosing the right words and tone is important and is referred to as how you 'phrase' your feedback. This is why the feedback sandwich is helpful, as you are telling the person more positive things than negative. If you know that the person you are feeding back to is easily upset, begin by enthusiastically mentioning the positive aspects. You could then move on to the negative aspects but refer back to the positive elements and always end by highlighting the positive parts, as shown in the previous example. You want to encourage the person to improve upon their previous efforts and the best way to do this is to give sensitive and constructive feedback so they can improve their work.

Sharing opinions

When discussing a subject, you may find yourself disagreeing with what others say. This is because everyone has their own individual opinions. For example, you may not agree with testing medicines on animals or have the same music taste as your peers, but this doesn't make your opinions wrong or others right. Opinions develop over time and others can influence your views (or not!). **Sharing opinions** is an important aspect of business, and it is vital that everyone is able to share their opinion before final decisions are made.

> **Activity**
>
> Working in pairs, look back at the TED talk activity (page 159) that you completed. Read your notes to your partner and ask them to give you some feedback using the concept of the feedback sandwich described above. Then do the same for your partner.

> **Key term**
>
> **Sharing opinions** A method of discussing different ideas to try to influence others

Encouragement

It is very important to encourage individuals by ensuring that you focus on the positive aspects of their work, which will give them the confidence to continue. With encouragement from others, they may be able to identify areas that they themselves could improve.

Establish ideas for further refinement

Accepting feedback from your peers or others gives you an opportunity to improve your pitch. Using this new information could enable you to see how other parts of your pitch could be altered or improved, which could be a bonus. However, it is important to be realistic about how much to change as you need to be aware of the time you might spend.

3.3 Review a practice pitch in order to plan for a professional pitch to an external audience

Having the opportunity to revisit and improve your pitch as a result of feedback received from others is a vital part of preparing for the actual pitch. We have discussed the different forms of feedback but how do you use this new information? First of all, you need to accept that the feedback that you have been given is 'constructive', i.e. it is intended to help you make improvements so you should not take the comments personally.

In the activity on page 162 you were asked to provide feedback after listening to a group make a pitch about a new children's drink. Some of the points that you were asked to comment upon were:

- What is the name of the drink?
- What did you think of the logo design?
- How did the presenters come across to you?
- Sum up your overall impression of the pitch.

> ### Activity
>
> In groups of three, choose one of the following topics to discuss. Your current top three:
>
> - music artists
> - video games
> - vloggers.
>
> Do you agree or disagree with each other's opinions? Explain why and feed back your findings to the rest of the class.

Activity

Read the following reviews of two different pitches for the new children's drink referred to in the activity on page 162.

Review 1

The name of the drink was 'Zoom' which I think is great because it will appeal to young children. It is a short and snappy name. The logo of a moon appearing within the name Zoom was very original. I do wonder if it will appeal to both boys and girls with a name like Zoom. I think that it will appeal more to boys. The presenters seemed to be very nervous which I was surprised at as the idea is very good. They read quite a bit so their eye contact was not very good. Sammy spoke very quietly. They could have smiled more, especially when saying the slogan 'Zoom your thirst' which was similar to 'quench your thirst' which appears in other adverts. I thought this was great. Maybe if they practised more and were more prepared with what they were going to say, this would help the nerves. The slides moved quite quickly so the timings should be improved. There were a few spelling mistakes also within the slides. In summary, it's a great idea for a product, they have a good logo and slogan but more work could be added into the pitch style.

$\rightarrow$

→

Review 2

The name of the drink was not very original, being called 'Strawberry Heaven' but I'm not sure if there is another drink called that that you can buy. The design of the logo was good as it was a strawberry heart as a strawberry is sort of a heart shape anyway. I think this is great as heaven is like a heart. The overall image of the drink was not very clear so I think that this should be improved. They should make the logo bigger and make the name stand out more on the bottle. I would also have a font of different writing – maybe something swirly but it must be easy to read. Both Emily and Julia spoke clearly while completing the pitch and had good eye contact. They didn't speak too fast or too slowly – it was just right! They had prepared their notes well and had put numbers in the corner of each of the notes so that they could keep track. This helped Julia when she dropped one of the notes as she could just put it back in the right place. I thought their overall pitch was good but they just need to change some of the design and explain this better within the pitch.

Questions

1 Do you think that the feedback given was fair in each case? Explain your answer.
2 Identify what each group needs to do to improve their pitches.

Answers to these questions are based upon your opinion. The group receiving your feedback can decide to take on board your comments or ignore them. Everyone has their own personal opinions on topics, which you may agree or disagree with, but with regard to feedback on your pitch, it is important to consider other's views.

The feedback gives the person the opportunity to improve their pitch but also highlights the importance of preparing for a pitch in the right way. Look back at the feedback that you received for your pitch on the children's drink. Would you change anything about it as a result of reading this feedback? Share your opinion with the class and justify your reasoning.

3.4 Deliver a professional pitch to an external audience

Delivering a pitch is an opportunity for people to communicate their business ideas to an audience who are interested in investing in a business venture. It is clear that a lot of preparation is required before reaching the stage of making a pitch. For example, a business would be advised to complete the following:

- consider the business idea
- build a customer profile
- undertake market research
- consider product design
- draw up costings
- consider risks

Stretch activity

Devise ten different top tips for creating the perfect pitch to help others. Each top tip should include an example to illustrate the meaning. Once completed, create a guide that other peers could use when preparing a pitch.

- write the pitch
- prepare visual aids
- practise the pitch
- review and alter the pitch as a result of feedback.

Once these different processes have been completed, a person or business would be ready to deliver a professional pitch to an audience. Pitching a business proposal will enable the business to demonstrate their organisational, preparation and communication skills. It is an opportunity to show all of the ideas to an audience who are there to learn about the ideas. It would be sensible for a business to remember to do the following:

- practise the pitch
- pack the resources and props required for the pitch in good time beforehand in preparation, and check them again on arrival
- get a good night's sleep
- make sure the presenter or presenters look professional
- arrive at the venue in plenty of time
- make sure the room is set up to the business's requirements
- take some deep breaths before starting a pitch, remembering to introduce the presenters
- keep calm and focused throughout the pitch, remembering to maintain eye contact with the audience to demonstrate confidence. This is the time for a business to show off their idea!
- always remember to thank the audience for listening
- invite questions from the audience and remember to think before answering. If a person is not sure of the answer, be honest and don't make up an answer that is incorrect.

After the business has completed a pitch, a review will normally happen. This could be a formal meeting which could be documented. The review will focus on all the positive aspects of the pitch and maybe some aspects that could have been completed in a different way.

Activity

The TV show *Dragons' Den* is famous for enabling people to pitch their business ideas to successful and well-known entrepreneurs. Watch three different pitches from the show and write down the main differences between each. What elements have you noted that you think will help you when you deliver your pitch? Are there any ideas that you think you could use within your pitch?

Test your knowledge

1 What is the difference between verbal and non-verbal skills?
2 Why is it important to rehearse a pitch?
3 Write a definition of constructive feedback.
4 What is a feedback sandwich?
5 How can you prepare answers to questions that you may be asked as part of your pitch?
6 Give five tips for delivering a pitch to an audience.

Read about it

www.thisismoney.co.uk/money/smallbusiness/article-4888320/Deborah-Meaden-tips-deliver-perfect-business-pitch.html – Advice on pitching a business from Deborah Meaden from Dragon's Den

LO4 Be able to review the strengths and weaknesses of a proposal and pitch

This final part of the course focuses on how to review a proposal and pitch using a variety of methods. You will learn how to review the strengths and weaknesses of both your business proposal and the pitch that you completed. Completing a review is an opportunity to learn from your experience, so you can use this knowledge to improve in future.

Teaching content

In this learning outcome you will:

4.1 Review a professional pitch to an external audience

4.2 Review a business proposal.

4.1 Review a professional pitch to an external audience

Reviewing a pitch after it has taken place is an important aspect of the pitching process. It enables you to focus on the positive and negative elements of a pitch and to consider what you might do differently next time.

Review a pitch, using a range of sources of evidence

There are a number of different ways that you can review a pitch. Using a mixture of these different sources of information to improve your ability to create and deliver a pitch will enhance your future opportunities when working in the world of business.

Self-assessment

Self-assessment is when you individually assess different aspects of your work. This could be preparation carried out before the pitch, your attitude towards the task, what went well, what didn't work so well and how you felt overall about the pitch. Self-assessment is a very useful method of reviewing, but in order for it to work you need to be honest with yourself. Nothing is perfect and there is always room for improvement. Give yourself the time and space to complete an honest self-assessment so that it is meaningful and your findings can then be used in the future.

Feedback from others

Part of Learning Outcome 3 focused on obtaining feedback from others, including your peers. (See pages 163–164 for an explanation of the feedback sandwich, how to phrase feedback to individuals, encourage others and share your own opinions.) Using different types of feedback can help you gain several different views on your pitch. Some of these views could be contradictory, for example, one person might say, 'I really liked the logo' while another person

Getting started

In groups of no more than four people, write down 15 words that describe how reviewing a proposal and pitch could help you to improve your performance in future. Share your words with the rest of the class.

Key term

Self-assessment Reviewing work that you have previously completed

167

could say 'I did not understand the logo idea, even when it was explained to me'. This demonstrates that people have different opinions. Some of the comments you may choose to ignore while others might give you the opportunity to alter something that you had not previously identified within the pitch. For example, if a member of your family says your conclusion does not really make sense, you could then discuss with them how to make it better. Perhaps it needs more focus or to highlight the main points made at the start.

Lessons learned from the practice pitch

Another source of evidence that can be used to help review a pitch is by using the experience of completing a practice pitch. Focus on the changes that need to be made and document them to provide you with a source of review. For example, perhaps your PowerPoint presentation was too fast to deliver information during your practice pitch and you had to alter the pitch as a result, in order to make sure the PowerPoint information was accessible to the audience.

Lessons learned from the professional pitch

Another source of evidence is reviews of the professional pitch. Verbal feedback from the audience could be recorded so that it can be viewed later on. The audience may also be given the opportunity to complete some written feedback, which can then be analysed after the pitch has taken place. The questions that the audience ask can also gauge their interest in the business proposal and this can be used as a source of evidence.

Activity

1 Ask your teacher to provide you with a piece of work that you completed at the start of the OCR Cambridge National in Enterprise and Marketing qualification. Look at this piece of work and complete a self-assessment on it. Consider what you think of its content, the language used and how it is presented. What would you do now to improve it? Be honest!

2 As a class, create a list of the most common mistakes that are made when creating a document. For example, writing the word 'form' instead of 'from', or writing 'there' instead of 'their'.

3 Identify three main lessons that you learned from completing your practice pitch. Contribute to a class discussion on this topic.

4 Write a blog that details your experience of completing a professional pitch in front of an audience. Include your top tips for delivering the perfect pitch to help others who may be preparing a business pitch.

Compare the outcomes of the pitch with the objectives

A business will often complete a review of a pitch which will focus on the positive aspects and on things that could have been improved. It could be in the form of a meeting. In preparation for such a meeting, the business may put together a document in advance for people who are attending the meeting which focuses on the following different themes:

- what went well
- what could have been improved
- the format of the pitch
- the content of the pitch
- visual aids designed for the purpose of the pitch
- the impact of the visual aids on the pitch
- timings of the pitch
- anticipation and preparation of responses to potential questions.

Asking colleagues to write down their thoughts and comments on the different themes outlined above will enable a discussion to take place with different views prepared in advance. This would mean that within the review meeting, everyone's views could be discussed and an action plan be devised for any other similar business opportunities that may arise in the future, so that staff could be fully prepared.

Reviewing your pitch using the bulleted list above will help you focus your thoughts and can be used as a checklist when reviewing a pitch.

Personal presentation skills

Communication

You have seen that preparation is the key to delivering a successful pitch to an audience. Preparation involves deciding upon the content, the visual aids and how you present your pitch. Mehrabain's communication model (page 156) shows that all three elements of this model are important. Communicating is not just the words that we speak but the actions we display, sometimes unknowingly! This can be in the form of both verbal and non-verbal communication (see pages 156–157). Reviewing the communication skills you demonstrated will enable you to improve these for future opportunities.

Activity

Go to the MindTools website and complete the communication quiz: **www.mindtools.com/pages/article/newCS_99.htm**

Do you agree with the interpretation for your score? Compare your answers with another member of your class.

Stretch activity

1   Quickly think of a great day that you recently experienced. Consider why this was the best day compared to other days. Describe the contents of the day from start to finish. Write down some prompts to help you.

2   Now describe this day to a partner. They will listen to the content and should focus on the communication skills that you demonstrate. Ask your partner to feed back to you the positive and negative aspects of your communication.

3   Once you have received feedback, think about what has been said. Do you agree with their summary of your communication skills?

169

Professionalism

How you present yourself to an audience is an important aspect of personal presentation skills. Dressing smartly and good personal hygiene indicates your professionalism. If you look untidy, it can give the impression that you do not care. A person may decide not to invest in your business if they think your untidy approach extends to the way you run your business.

Ability to answer questions from the audience

You may not want your audience to ask lots of questions, but it is vital that investors can obtain further information from you. You may surprise yourself with the responses that you are able to give, so do not shy away. Staying calm in stressful situations is not always easy, but with practice and the support of others, the better the experience will be. You might even enjoy it!

Future developments/recommendations for further refinement

When any kind of project or business has been completed or launched, it is a good idea to think about how the idea can be developed further. Businesses are always looking to improve or develop new products (known as **product development**), in order to enjoy repeat custom and differentiate them from their competitors.

 Key term

Product development
When a business takes an existing product as its basis for creating new products

Activity

The images below show two famous products – KitKat and Tango – that have been developed over time to create new product ranges.

1 Research the different products that are now available as a result of these developments.
2 What other examples of product development can you think of?

Recognising that further developments or improvements can always be made is an important aspect of product development. As individuals, we develop and change our opinions and this happens in the business world too. No matter how many presentations or pitches you complete, there is always room for improvement.

Activity

Jamie and Jasper have been asked to complete a pitch to their class. Think about the preparation that will be required, the visual aids that will be needed and the decisions to be made on who says what. Then decide if the following statements are true or false.

Statement	True/False
Jamie and Jasper should wait a few days before starting to plan their work.	
Jamie and Jasper should discuss between them what is involved in this work.	
The boys should complete each part of the work separately and compare notes at the end.	
It is important that one person completes more work than the other to show who is in charge of the pitch.	
Visual aids are not necessary if clear explanations are given in the pitch.	
Jamie and Jasper should practise their presentation or pitch several times before it is delivered.	
Jamie gets very nervous and finds eye contact difficult in any situation. He should therefore not worry about this part of the work and just look at the floor or his notes during the presentation.	
The visual aids don't need to be checked again on the day of the presentation if they were working the day before.	
It is natural to feel nervous in this situation.	
Jasper and Jamie need to raise their voices when delivering their pitch so that everyone in the audience can hear them.	
The boys don't have to give the audience the opportunity to ask questions if they don't want to answer them.	

4.2 Review a business proposal

This unit has focused on learning about the knowledge and skills needed to review a business proposal. Businesses will need to ensure that their staff have the right knowledge and skills when reviewing any new business idea. A business will put together a plan of what information will be required.

- **product proposal** – a description of the product and its unique selling point, etc.
- **pricing strategy** – the pricing methods that they intend to adopt to try to obtain sales
- **brand** – the brand personality, identity and image which is individual to the product
- **promotional plan** – the different promotional methods that were created to sell the product
- **relevance and appeal to the customer profile** – research that shows why customers will want to purchase the product.

Earlier in this unit you looked at how useful self-assessment can be as a form of feedback (see page 167). People that write blogs about pitching to investors are using a form of public self-assessment, because they have used their own words to describe their experiences. Although their individual experiences and outcomes may be different, they all chose to use a pitch to try to launch their product or service ideas.

Reviewing your proposal using feedback from others and your experiences of practicing and delivering a professional pitch will ensure that you have balanced and varied views on the work that you have produced.

Stretch activity

Justify your responses to the task and advise Jamie and Jasper what is the right thing to do in each situation.

Activity

The experiences of business bloggers such as Jack Monroe or successful business people such as Lord Alan Sugar can be found on the internet.

1 Research one blogger and one successful business person to find out the highs and lows of their business experiences. Make notes on their thoughts.

2 How did these experiences help them in their career?

3 Share the highlights with the rest of the class.

171

Feedback from others could include:

- family members, customers or representatives of your customer profile
- the people that you pitched your practice business proposal to, as this is just as important as the actual professional pitch. Their comments will help you justify any changes you made to your presentation
- peers, because they understand the pressures you are under and can provide constructive criticism
- commercial contacts – people who can provide a critical business review of your proposal, as they may be able to spot errors or unrealistic targets which others may not.

 Case study

The final part of a business proposal is to think about the future for the product. Read the following information which has been adapted from the experiences of people who have completed pitches to an audience.

Preparation

Preparing for a pitch focuses the person or people delivering the pitch to answer different questions which can help to explain how the product could develop over time. What does the business actually do? Where is the business going? What is the main brand? (Is there a brand?) What are the figures involved in the business? These are key questions that the person delivering the pitch will need to be able to answer. Answering such questions will give the presenter clarity as to what to say and helps them focus on the future.

Listen and react to the feedback

The people listening to the pitch are there to hear about the business's ideas and support the business. The feedback given from the audience can help the people giving the pitch think differently about how to approach the business in the future. The audience members will have different areas of expertise and by listening to their advice the business may get new ideas for the way in which they develop, promote and package their products. All opinions are important and listening to the feedback from

a pitch and reacting to it can impact on the success of a product.

Negotiating

Negotiating does not always come naturally to people. The audience members listening to a pitch, such as the Dragons on Dragons' Den, will have the upper hand as they are business people who thrive on negotiating. Not everyone will have these skills. A business might receive two or three offers of financial help as a result of delivering a successful pitch. Having a choice of offers gives a business the opportunity to grow their businesses. However, those involved in negotiating will need to be able to think quickly on their feet to work out if the offers are worth considering given the direction that they want their business to go. Sometimes in this situation people have walked away from the offer and preferred to grow their business another way. It is hard to predict the questions that an audience may ask but it is worth practicing some role plays of different scenarios of negotiating so that the business is prepared for this aspect of a pitch.

Take advantage of new business experiences

Businesses have said how participating in a pitch has helped them in many different ways. If the pitch was for a television programme or a local business group or competition, the business expertise in the audience and

→ publicity of the event has often given the business new opportunities and experiences. Some participants have said that enquiries and sales for the products increased dramatically both locally and nationally, and in some circumstances internationally, after the event. This includes both businesses who accepted offers from the pitch or ones that declined offers. Both types said that the publicity that they received from the event really did give them more of a platform to promote their business as they could mention in their advertising that they had been part of an event.

Having confidence

Pitching a business idea can be a very pressured situation but what will get any person through the experience is having confidence in the business idea. If the person presenting does not demonstrate confidence in the pitch, the audience may interpret this as not having confidence in the product or service which could be a disaster. For people who have had experience of this situation, they have stated that it is important to believe in yourself and the business. Having the ability to accept or walk away from any offers that may or may not help the business at the end of a pitch also shows confidence in the business ideas.

Question

Using this information, how do you think that you could further develop your business proposal?

Explain your reasons.

Test your knowledge

1 How can preparing answers to potential questions help when delivering a pitch to an audience?

2 Name two different forms of evidence that could be used when reviewing a pitch.

3 If you were to offer advice to a friend who has to deliver a pitch, what would you say?

4 What are the benefits of reviewing a business proposal?

Read about it

www.tutor2u.net/business/reference/promotion-introduction – Outline of the different methods of promotion

www.director.co.uk/9672-dragons-den-do-the-deals-ever-work/ – Article looking at business successes and failures from Dragons Den

https://beeline.co/blogs/news/here-is-what-happened-since-weve-been-at-dragons-den – A company explains what happened to them after their appearance on Dragons Den

www.tutor2u.net/business/reference/planning-a-new-business – Revision guidance on planning a new business

Glossary

Aesthetics How a product looks or feels

Banner advertising A form of advertising containing product or service information that moves across a screen

Brand How a business is identified by others, such as customers and competitors

Brand image The visual elements of a brand created by a business, such as its logo or a slogan

Break-even The point at which a business makes no profit and no loss. It is the point at which total costs equal total revenue

Business angel Wealthy entrepreneur who provides a business owner with a substantial sum of money to help set up a business; in return they receive a proportion of the business's profits

Cash flow The movement of money into and out of a business

Competitive pricing Setting a price that is similar to that of a local competitor

Constructive feedback Giving your opinion of something (both positive and negative) and suggesting ways in which improvements could be made

Contribution The amount left over after variable costs have been subtracted from sales revenue. Contribution per unit is calculated as selling price per unit minus variable cost per unit

Copyright Provides legal ownership to original pieces of creative work

Crowdfunding Groups of investors that join together to offer funding to a business

Customer profile Researching vital information about customers to ensure that products and services appeal to them

Customer retention The ability of a business to keep customers

Design An initial sketch or drawing for a product that can be developed over time

Direct marketing A method of advertising that is targeted at specific customers

Economic manufacture Making sure the costs involved in producing a product are appropriate to that product and no money is wasted during the manufacturing process

Extension strategies Actions a business can take to extend the life of a product and increase sales

Feedback sandwich Three different parts of constructive feedback – the two slices of bread represent positive feedback with the filling of the sandwich being made up of constructive criticism

Fixed costs Costs that remain unchanged when the output of a business changes

Focus group A group of people who participate in a discussion about products and services

Formal language Less personal language that is used in business and other professional settings, that often features a variety of words, including technical terms and jargon

Franchise A business where the franchisor (the owner of the business idea) grants a licence (the franchise) to another business (the franchisee) to operate their brand or business idea

Function The job which a product or service is designed to do

Functional area A department that plays a specific role within an organisation and whose employees carry out a particular aspect of the work of the organisation. For example, in the finance area, the employees will all have skills in accounting

Informal language Language that is used in conversation with friends and family and which may include slang or abbreviated words

Investor A wealthy individual listening to a pitch who may loan money to a business to help get it started in return for a share of the profits

Limited liability The business owners are only liable for the debts of a business up to the amount of money they have invested in the business

Loan Long-term source of finance offered by banks, building societies or other financial institutions

Market A place where buyers and sellers come together to trade goods and services

Market/customer segmentation The division of a market into groups or segments

Market research The actions of a business to gather information about customers' needs and wants

Market segmentation Dividing the market for a product or service into sections or segments in order to target particular types of customers

Market share The section of a market controlled by a particular business

Partnership A business that is owned and controlled by two or more partners

Patent Provides legal ownership of new inventions and prevents these being used or produced by others

Personal savings Money that a business owner invests in their own business

Pitch A method of communicating and presenting a business proposal to an audience

Pop-ups Mini adverts that appear on screen to temporarily distract the audience and draw them away from what they are looking at, before disappearing

Potential customers People who are interested in the products or services that you sell and who may be persuaded to buy them

Price penetration Introducing a product at a lower price than usual to attract customers, then gradually increasing the price over time

Price skimming Introducing a product at a high price then gradually lowering the price over time

Pricing strategies Different methods of pricing used by businesses to encourage customers to purchase their products

Primary (field) research Gathering data and information that has not been collected before

Product development When a business takes an existing product as its basis for creating new products

Product lifecycle Shows the journey of a product from its development and launch to its eventual removal from sale

Professionalism Consistently displaying appearance and conduct of the highest quality and is associated with the impression that is given to others when working in a business

Profit A financial gain. Profit is calculated as the difference between total revenue and total costs

Promotion The different methods used by a business to ensure that customers are aware of its products and services

Prototype A physical object produced from a design to determine whether it meets the original concept and can be developed further. Often many prototypes have to be produced before the final idea works

Psychological pricing Setting a price that appears attractive to a customer

Qualitative data Data based on the opinions of those being asked

Quantitative data Data collected that is based on facts or numbers; it is usually easier to analyse than qualitative data

Revenue The money a business earns from selling goods or providing services

Sampling A method of selecting consumers in order to gain their opinions on a product or service. Types of sampling include random, cluster, quota and convenience

Secondary (desk) research Gathering data and information that has already been collected before

Self-assessment Reviewing work that you have previously completed

Sharing opinions A method of discussing different ideas to try to influence others

Small business grants Sums of money available from various charities or the government to help individuals set up a business

Sole trader A business that is owned and controlled by one person

Target market A particular group of customers at which a good or service is aimed

Total costs Calculated by adding together all the business's costs for a particular level of output

Total revenue The total amount of money earned at a particular output level. It is calculated as selling price per unit × output level (number of sales)

Unique selling point (USP) The key features that make a product or service different to others in the market

Unlimited liability The business owner(s) are personally liable for the debts of the business in the event that the business cannot pay them

Variable costs Costs that vary directly with (and are dependent on) the level of output

Verbal skills Using the voice to communicate with others in such a way that they understand the message that is being conveyed

Test your knowledge answers

R064 Enterprise and marketing concepts

LO1 Understand how to target a market

1 Market research involves finding out information about the market in which the business organisation operates.

2 Sources could include:

- Interviews
- Observations
- Questionnaires
- Focus groups
- Consumer trials.

3 Five from:

- Age
- Gender
- Occupation
- Income
- Geographic
- Lifestyle

4 Advantages include:

- Segmentation ensures customer needs are matched and met. By focusing on one particular area, businesses are more likely to meet the needs and wants of their customers and therefore the business will increase sales and profits.

- Segmentation makes it more likely that customers will keep returning to the business for their purchases. This will lead to increased customer retention.

- Market segmentation allows for targeted marketing, as a business organisation is able to deliver its marketing and advertisements to customers who will have a key interest in the product being offered.

5 Benefits of research include:

- Helping a business to understand the market and to reduce risk – comprehensive market research will allow a business organisation to understand the needs of the market and then provide goods and services to meet those needs.

- To gain customers' views and understand their needs – this allows managers to make informed decisions. Market research allows customers to discuss their views, needs and wants, etc., in terms of products and services offered. This information provides a business organisation with a comprehensive overview of what needs to be produced and sold in order to meet customers' expectations.

- To inform product development and to promote the organisation – comprehensive and accurate market research reduces the risk of launching new or updated products. By completing appropriate research, the business can reduce this risk of launching a product that customers do not want.

LO2 Understand what makes a product or service financially viable

1 Fixed costs are costs that remain unchanged when the output of a business organisation changes. Variable costs are costs that vary directly with the level of output.

2 Examples include:
- Fixed costs – rent, loan repayments, advertising, salaries.
- Variable costs - costs that vary directly with the level of output such as stock, raw materials and packaging costs.

3 Break-even point is the point at which a business organisation makes no profit and no loss. It is the point at which total costs equal total revenue. It is calculated as the difference between the total revenue and total costs.

4 Profit is a financial gain. It is calculated as the difference between the total revenue and total costs. Contribution is the amount left over after variable costs have been taken away from sales revenue. Contribution per unit is calculated as selling price per unit less variable cost per unit.

5 Break-even information is used by business organisations to determine how many units a business organisation needs to sell in order to cover its costs and not make a loss and can form part of a business organisation's business plan. The break-even graph provides a visual image of the break-even point of a business organisation. This is particularly important for individuals that are not accountants.

6 Profit = Sales revenue less total costs
$$50\,000 = 300\,000 - \text{total costs}$$
$$\text{Total costs} = £250\,000$$

LO3 Understand what makes a product or service financially viable

1 The main stages are:
- Development – a business organisation will research and develop the product before it is made available for sale to the customer. Product testing and trials take place.
- Introduction –the new product is launched. The business organisation advertises the product heavily to improve customer knowledge of the product and tries to encourage sales. The company will be making low profits and possibly losing money and will have a low market share.
- Growth – customers are familiar with the product, sales increase at their fastest rate and profits will rise. Competitors may enter the market.
- Maturity – sales have reached their highest. The number of new customers is likely to be reducing and growth is limited. Other business organisations may have entered the market or the number of products available may mean the market is saturated.
- Decline – sales of the product will begin to fall. Customers will no longer be interested and may have switched to newer alternative products. The business organisation will not advertise the product and will eventually remove it from sale.

2 Strategies could include:
- New advertising campaigns: the aim of a new advertising campaign is to attract both new and existing customers.
- New pricing strategies: to try to give an increased sense of value, a business organisation may reduce the selling price of its products and services.
- New product features: businesses might add extra features and functions, for example, fast food restaurants now offer drive through facilities, table service or the option to order on screen.

3 A unique selling point is the key product feature that separates that product from its competitors. Examples of products with USPs include:
- Car performance – BMW/Porsche
- Branding – Nike
- Design – Apple iPhone/iPod.

4 The design mix model is a way of considering the variables that contribute to successful product design. These are:
- Function – any product must be able to do the job for which it was designed
- Economic manufacture – a product must be financially viable and cost effective to produce. Materials appropriate to the product need to be used.

- Aesthetics – this is how a product looks or feels, which is very important when trying to sell goods or services.

5 The effects of the different stages are as follows:
- During a decline period, business organisations suffer from a decrease in sales and there is little or no demand for new products or services. A business is therefore unlikely to develop new products during this time.
- During a growth period, customers have more money to spend and are likely to want to purchase new goods or services. Business organisations will therefore develop and sell new products.
- On reaching the boom period, customer spending is at its highest and business organisations are likely to introduce and sell a wide range of new products.
- During a recession, customers have very little money to spend on luxury goods, so business organisations need to consider developing cheaper products.

LO4 Understand how to attract and retain customers

1 A business will price its product by working out what it costs to buy or make the product and then adding the amount of profit they would like to make.

2 Competitive pricing is when a business organisation sets a price that is similar to that of a local competitor.

3 Methods could include:
- Leaflets as they are low cost and can be targeted to customers in the local area.
- Online advertising, for example paying for adverts on search engine results pages or on social networking sites or paying for pop-up adverts on websites.
- The retailer could use a newspaper – they would need to decide whether they want to advertise in free and local newspapers, where advertisements are relatively cheap, or large adverts in national newspapers, which are extremely expensive.

4 Sales promotions could include:
- Buy one get one free
- Competitions
- Point of sale material, for example by the tills in supermarkets.

5 Excellent customer service will:
- Provide word of mouth promotion
- Improve business reputation
- Encourage repeat business
- Set the business apart from competitors
- Provide brand awareness
- Ensure customer loyalty and encourage customers to purchase from the business organisation in the future

LO5 Understand factors for consideration when starting up a business

1 A franchise is a business organisation where the franchisor (the owner of the business idea) grants a licence (the franchise) to another business (the franchisee), so they can sell their brand or business idea. The franchisor owns the business idea and decides how the business will be operated and run.

2 A sole trader is a business owned and controlled by one individual whereas a partnership is a business organisation that is owned and controlled by two or more individuals.

3 Unlimited liability means the sole trader would need to pay the business's organisation's debts if they could not be paid.

4 Sources of capital might include:
- Own savings –money that the owner has invested into their own business.
- Friends and family – friends and family are often willing to lend business owners money to start up their business organisation.
- Loans – loans are offered by banks, building societies or other financial institutions. The financial institution will ask to see evidence that the business will be able to repay the amount due and are usually repaid over three to ten years. In return for lending the money, the lending institution will charge

interest. This will need to be repaid along with the amount of money borrowed.

- Crowdfunding – this is a newer method of finance for new business organisations. Crowdfunding asks a group or 'crowd' of investors for funding, so instead of one person investing there could be 100 investors all willing to invest smaller amounts of money. This shares the risk of investment in case the business organisation does not succeed.

- Small business grants – these may be available from various charities or the government to help individuals to set up. There is usually set criteria that need to be met in order to access the grants. The business owner will need to have a clear business plan and model of how they see the business organisation being operating and progressing in the future.

- Business angels – wealthy entrepreneurs who provide a substantial sum of money to set up a business organisation in return for a proportion of the business organisations capital. The business angel takes high personal risk by investing but if the business organisation is successful, they would achieve large returns.

5   Reasons why a business organisation needs to prepare a business plan include:

- To clarify a business idea to others (e.g. to secure funding)

- To help identify potential problems (e.g. financial shortages)

- To be able to manage their cash flow

- To measure progress towards goals (e.g. timescales, sales forecasts)

LO6 Understand different functional activities needed

1   A functional area is a set of employees who all have similar skills. For example, in the finance area, the employees will all have skills in accounting.

2   A marketing department or area is used to promote or advertise products and services. As an area, they will gain an understanding of the needs and wants of the business organisation's customers. A marketing department or area is responsible for promotional activities that will help to generate awareness and sales and try to ensure that the business organisation grows.

3   The operations department deals with the production processes within a business organisation. They are responsible for overseeing, designing and controlling how production processes work and will be responsible for the managing how the production processes are controlled. This department is also responsible for ensuring both quality and stock/inventory control and review the logistics and make sure that all equipment/machinery is available when required.

4   Human resource department activities include:

- Recruitment and selection of employees

- Training and development of employees

- Performance management of employees

- Responsibility for health and safety in the workplace

- Ensuring compliance with employment legislation

5   The finance department controls all monetary aspects of a business's operation. They will consider how financial resources are allocated to different departments and ensure there is sufficient cash within the business organisation to pay all of their bills. At various points in the year, the finance department will report on the financial position and performance of the business organisation. They will prepare detailed reports assessing profitability, liquidity etc. and then analyse the reports.

R065 Design a business proposal

LO1 Be able to identify the customer profile for a business challenge

1   The method a business will use to divide customers into different groups (segments).

2   Segmenting the market helps a business to target individual products or brands to

the customer groups (segments) in order to sell them. Knowing information about the different segments means that the choice of advertising, packaging etc. enables the product to be refined which will then appeal to the known audience. If the customers like it, sales should be high within the segmentation.

3 The products will appeal to the target market and the product should sell to the target market meaning profits will increase for the business. Increased knowledge of the segmentation will help the business design more appealing products for future sales.

4 Any three of the following:
- Age
- Gender
- Occupation
- Income
- Lifestyle

5 Market segmentation can help a business create a customer profile because they will have more knowledge about its customers from the completed research to build up a profile of its likely customers. This research might include details of where such a customer might live, occupation and income level, how old they are, lifestyle choices and what they like to buy. The business then uses this customer profile to target its products at these types of potential customers.

6 Customer profiling is when a business uses knowledge of its customers and research into market segmentation to build up an image or profile of its likely customers.

LO2 Complete market research to aid decisions

1 Primary research is when a business researches information for its own use and for a specific reason. The information required does not yet exist, so will be original for that business. Secondary research is research that already exists and has been produced by another party. It can take many forms, including competitor research, articles in magazines or newspapers and government and industry reports.

2 Market research is a method of gathering data for a particular purpose to help a business make a business decision.

3 Any three of the following:
- Questionnaire
- Focus groups
- Interviews
- Surveys
- Test marketing
- Observations

4 Any four of the following:
- Internet
- Existing market research
- Newspaper articles
- Magazine articles
- Published data, for example company reports, reports by governments, local councils and industry bodies

5 Any reasonable example of an open question, for example 'describe your ideal day out'.

6 Sampling involves selecting a certain number of people, chosen from a particular group, and asking their opinions on a product or service. The results of this research are assumed to reflect the opinions of the group as a whole

7 Random sampling is when people are chosen by chance (random) to gain for example the opinion and views of a cross section of people.

Cluster sampling is when a research group is separated into smaller groups which are known as clusters such as geographically to gain the views and opinions of each cluster.

Quota sampling when the population is separated into a number of different groups who share the same characteristics such as age, gender, hobbies, interests etc.

8 You could use a primary research method and visit the supermarket and complete a questionnaire that you had devised to find out the costs of a two litre bottle of water in various brands. You could also go online and look up the costs of all the different two litre bottles of water that the supermarket sells. The issue with this method is that some of the varieties on the website might not be available in the shop.

LO3 Be able to develop a design proposal for a business challenge

1 A draft design is the initial product design process which can be used to produce a prototype, which is the first version of a physical product using the design.

2 This is the first and most crucial stage of the product design process because seeing a sketch or a picture of a design can bring it to life.

3 A mind map provides a visual summary of your ideas for a product with the product idea appearing in the centre of the diagram with other aspects drawn around the central product idea. These are linked back to the product idea and each other with lines or arrows. Mood boards are used by a designer to record all their visual ideas such as images, sketches, materials and colours in one place. They enable the designer to review all their different ideas and then select the key ones for their product design.

4 SCAMPER stands for:

- Substitute
- Put to another
- Combine
- Eliminate
- Adapt
- Reverse
- Modify

5 The hats are:

- White hat – they will look at the information or data that they have to help understand the market, for example.
- Red hat – they will look at the problems associated with an idea and rely on their gut instinct as well as considering how people may respond.
- Black hat – they will focus on the issues that could cause a problem and the things that might go wrong with the idea.
- Yellow hat – they will think about the best aspects of everything, so have the power of positive thinking.
- Green hat – they will think about the future and where an idea might lead as well as being creative and creating solutions to any issues.
- Blue hat – they bring all the coloured hat ideas together and will manage the process and maintain control.

6 SWOT stands for:

- Strengths
- Opportunities
- Weaknesses
- Threats

7 A SWOT analysis enables a business to look at a design critically and assess the product. A product design then can be altered according to the outcomes.

LO4 Be able to review whether a business proposal is viable

1

	Explanation of terms
Cost per unit	The accurate costs involved in making each individual product such as raw materials, packaging, delivery, staff wages/salaries, overhead costs and advertising. This helps a business to determine the final selling price of a product.
Profit per unit	The amount of money that a business makes after all costs have been paid for.
Total costs	Total costs are found when the fixed and variable costs are added together: Total costs = Fixed cost + Variable costs
Total profit	Total profit is the amount of money that a business will receive from selling the number of products it has made that are then sold to the customers. The calculation for total profit is: Total profit = Total revenue – Total costs

2 Fixed costs are costs that do not change such as rent and insurance. Other examples could be water and power (electricity and gas), council rates, machinery, tools and specialist equipment.

Variable costs change according to a business's level of output such as raw materials and manpower.

3 Psychological pricing makes the customer think the product is cheaper than it really is, for example the product is priced at 99p instead of £1.00. There is 1p difference in price but it might seem much cheaper to a customer.

Price skimming might be used by a business when introducing a new product to the market so it does not face competition. A high price will be set to maximise profits before other competitors try to produce similar products and start to move into the market.

4 Break-even is the level of output at which total costs equal total revenue. A business makes no profit and no loss at this point.

5 The formula for break-even is: Break-even point (in units) =

$$\frac{\text{Fixed costs}}{\text{Selling price per unit} - \text{Variable cost per unit}}$$

6 Break-even helps a business to determine how many units it needs to sell in order to cover its costs and not make a loss. It can help a business to set targets for the sales team, determine if the business can afford a loan and can also form part of a business plan. Accountants may use break-even information to see how different sales levels will affect an organisation's profits.

7 Risks might include:

- Losing money – if a product that is launched does not sell at the expected level, the money that has been invested by the business will be lost.

- Overspending the budget – if a business does not keep within the agreed budget, this will mean the business makes less profit per item affecting the break-even point.

8 Copyright is there to protect the owner's ideas. If a business owns the copyright for a product or idea, it enables them to change the idea, share it, sell it or rent it, and prevent people from using it without permission.

9 If a business patents a product it means they alone can legally produce and market the product for a set amount of time. This means the original inventor can take advantage of the hopefully increasing sales of the product before other companies are able to produce a version of the product that is similar, but not exactly the same.

10 Having a trademark protects your unique brand from being copied by other businesses. It could be the name of a product or the service that a business owns. All trademarks have to be registered. If someone does try to use the trademark, legal action can be sought.

RO66 Market and pitch a business proposal

LO1 Develop a brand identity and promotional plan

1 A brand is how a business can be identified. A brand can be recognised from a famous phrase, an image or a particular identity.

2 If a brand is successful, then customers learn to trust the brand and will purchase new products produced under that brand. A brand is not just its name, but how customers regard the business as a whole.

3 A brand image is how a business demonstrates its company values and messages by developing products and/or services that are appropriate both now and into the future for their customers. These elements will form the strategy that a business uses to create its brand image.

A brand personality refers to the techniques a business uses to present its ideas to customers such as advertising campaigns that are bright and eye-catching or soft and calming depending on the products/services.

4 A brand adds value as customers learn to trust the brand as a result of their past experiences with the product or service. When a brand image is damaged due to bad publicity this can have a negative effect on the business.

5 This identifies the six main elements of brand identity which are: physique, personality, relationship, culture, reflection, self-image. They were identified by Jean-Noel Kapferer who was a branding specialist.

6 A logo is used to help customers identify a business easily by a symbol, picture or font that represents the business.

7 A slogan is a series of words which always appears within an advertisement and will form part of the product or service over a long period of time. A strapline is normally three or four words that are related to the business appearing at the bottom of an advertisement in some form, demonstrating the business's values and personality.

8 Examples could include:
- *Fabletics* by Kate Hudson
- *Goop* by Gwyneth Paltrow
- *Devonne* by Demi Lovato

9 Unique selling point

10 Promotional objectives are the targets that a business wants to achieve as a result of the promotions used to advertise a product.

11 Examples may include:
- Flyers
- Leaflets
- Billboards
- Online advertising
- Social media platforms
- Promotional emails
- SMS texts

LO2 Be able to plan a pitch for a proposal

1 The message that a business wants to get across to the audience about a business proposal to gain support for the idea.

2 A pitch needs to be planned to ensure that all the important information is included for the audience to hear. A structure for a pitch will normally be an introduction, main content and a conclusion.

3 An objective of a pitch is establishing what it is you are trying to achieve, such as communicating a message to an audience. Objectives are the different steps taken to ensure the message is communicated.

4 Examples could include:
- PowerPoint presentations
- Handouts

5 Looking professional and being dressed appropriately when delivering a pitch can give the presenter confidence to perform well.

6 The structure of a pitch will normally contain an introduction, main content and a conclusion.

7 Inviting questions will give investors the opportunity to find out more about what they have just heard.

LO3 Be able to pitch a proposal to an audience

1 Verbal skills are the use of the voice to communicate with others in such a way that they understand the message that is being conveyed. Non-verbal skills are the actions that we display as a form of communication such as body language, eye contact and gestures.

2 Rehearsing a pitch will show whether the information that you are trying to get across is too much or too little for the time allocated to the pitch, and will show you what needs to be altered or perfected.

3 Constructive feedback is a method of way of giving an opinion of a presentation or a pitch (positive or negative) so that it can be improved.

4 A feedback sandwich is three different parts of constructive feedback – the two slices of bread represent positive feedback with the filling of the sandwich being made up of constructive criticism.

5 Ask people who listen to you practicing your pitch to write questions that they think people will ask after seeing your pitch.

6 Tips might include:
- Practise your reviewed pitch the night before
- Pack the resources and props required for the pitch the night before
- Get a good night's sleep
- Make sure you look professional
- Arrive at the venue in plenty of time

LO4 Be able to review the strengths and weaknesses of a proposal and pitch

1 It can keep the presenter calm enabling them to answer confidently. This can give a positive impression to the audience.

2 Answers could include self-assessment and feedback from others.

3 Student's own answer based on the advice given in Unit RO66.

4 Reviewing a proposal using feedback from others and reflecting on own personal experiences of delivering a pitch will ensure that the overall proposal is balanced, looks professional and achieves the original objectives that were set.

Index